WORKING the TABLE

An Indie Author's Guide to Conventions

Published by Clockwork Dragon Books
www.clockworkdragon.net

First Printing, March 2016

No writers were seriously harmed in the making of this book. The damaged books mentioned, however, were completely trashed. We're both scarred for life.

ISBN: 978-1-944334-03-1

WORKING the TABLE

An Indie Author's Guide to Conventions

LEE FRENCH
JEFFREY COOK

Clockwork Dragon Books

Dedication

For the people who told us we had to make this book happen, each in their own ways: Brad Wheeler, Angela Korra'ti, Pamela Cowan, and Thomas Gondolfi. Extra special thanks to Madison Keller and her living room floor.

Table of Contents

Introduction

Jeff: This book didn't start with Lee and me. Plenty of projects and books have, but not this one. This came from people we've worked with telling us we needed to write this.

The push came from other authors and other vendors who've seen how we set up our table, how we push each other's books, and how we come into a convention—and then work said convention like we have a plan.

We're not best-selling authors (yet). But we are people who, a couple of years into our publishing career, are consistently making money selling books at conventions. In some ways, I'd argue, that's more useful to the average indie author who is venturing into the world of conventions and live events than the bestseller who is years removed from having to work tooth-and-nail for every sale.

We've learned from those with more experience than us, observed the ups and downs of other booths, gotten plenty of good advice, and also learned plenty of things we didn't want to do. This book helps pass on some of those lessons.

We work an average of 2.5 events a month or so, in all sorts of different conditions. We've worked huge comic-cons, small conventions, local fairs, and done the road trips.

In all of that, we've developed a coherent plan for setup and selling that takes advantage of both of our talents and helps us succeed at a higher level than either of us would alone.

This book also goes into some of that—and why we think it works.

So, for who I am: I'm the clockwork side of Clockwork Dragon. The term came from my first series, the *Dawn of Steam* trilogy of epistolary steampunk novels, and from my being an author and organizer for Writerpunk Press's charity anthologies. I also write YA Fantasy and Sci-fi.

My biggest strength in terms of what I bring to my business partnership with Lee is networking. She makes fun of the amount of times that we're having a discussion about what would be nice to have and I can say "I know a guy…" I host multi-author events, helped put together a series of charity anthologies that have full editing teams and art teams, and do a lot of the panels and public-speaking side of things.

Lee: I'm the dragon half of this partnership. My first series, a trilogy of superhero action stories called *Maze Beset*, features a main character whose superpower allows him to become a swarm of tiny dragons. Those three books are titled *Dragons In Pieces*, *Dragons In Chains*, and *Dragons In Flight*. It's possible I'm a little obsessed with flying lizards. I also write several kinds of fantasy, including YA, and science fiction. Dragons always seem to pop up, one way or another.

My strengths for this team are largely logistical and organizational. I'm good with setting things up, tearing things down, coming up with new displays, creating promotional art, and determining what works and what doesn't for the physical side of our tables. I do a lot of the non-glamorous background dirty work, handling money, paperwork, and obnoxious details, including collecting data and analyzing it.

In our particular case, because Jeff has a physical disability, the fact I have a car that can carry all our stuff and I can drive for long periods of time is also quite helpful. This also happens to be the primary reason we first started working together.

What we hope to do with this book is make the vendor rooms we work in more successful, more pleasant places to be, and more fun for everyone. When the vendors are happy, everyone is happy.

What is Soft Selling?

Lee: Something Jeff and I both feel strongly about is the Soft Sell. You'll see this term repeated throughout this book. It's the core component of our overall philosophy for book events and essential to understand if you want to use this book effectively. Later, we'll delve into the why and how. For now, we present an overview.

Jeff: When you go to a car dealership, a salesman will probably approach you right away. They'll make sure you know all about the merchandise, their deals, and what they think is important. Likewise, when you go to conventions, you'll see people, including authors, pressing their books at people, calling out actively to passers-by, or leaving their booth to approach people moving through the vendor hall. Those approaches are Hard Sells.

By contrast, if you go to the hardware store, you're likely to spend most of the time perusing on your own. Employees may ask "Can I help you with something?" or make sure you know they're available, but the assumption is that you know what you want. There's an information desk in many of them. In areas requiring expertise, the better stores have employees who are knowledgeable about products in the area they're working, and can tell you more or help you, but that's the extent of their assumptions. You're there because you want or need something at that store, and their role is to facilitate matching you up with what that is. They're unlikely to follow you around, or press advertising at you. Odds are, the shelves are labeled with their current deals and items they want to emphasize.

That's your goal with the Soft Sell. Make an environment people want to approach, with knowledgeable people on hand who are engaged and interested in what they're doing without being pushy. People in the vendor area at conventions are there because they're considering buying something. Your goal is for them to want to approach you and your table.

Another important point about the example used for explanation: when you engage customers with soft selling, you're not setting out to sell any particular book. You're not pushing your newest book at people who come by, or trying to convince people that you know what they'll enjoy. This is especially true if you're working with other authors, or have other people's books on the table. Your goal is to be customer-centric, trying to match customers up with something that will interest them.

Finally, think of the car dealer example. There are reasons the people who sell things on commission, and especially car dealers, tend to have a bad reputation. They may be good at moving merchandise, but they often make people uncomfortable in the process. While people are at the table, you want to maintain a comfortable atmosphere and let the customer's needs/wants drive the majority of the conversation.

Writing Books

Lee: Before you can sell books, you have to write and publish them. In this section, we discuss what it takes to get to that point. This is not intended to be a list of instructions for how to accomplish the minutia of self-publishing, but rather an overview of the mindset and skills necessary to get from an idea to a finished product.

Discipline

Jeff: This is a tough one, and one I'm still working on, certainly. If you're going to be successful as an author, or any type of artist, you need to treat it like a job. If you want to spend three years crafting your book and support your writing hobby with a regular day job, that's cool. You should definitely do that. If your goal is to make money vending at conventions, the people sharing the table need to collectively have a fair amount of work out.

You need to produce regularly. Find or make the time in your schedule to write. Prioritize it over other things in your life. Video games, television time, keeping your weekends free to hang out with friends—there's nothing wrong with any of those. However, they may need to be limited, or used as rewards in doses, if you're going to try to put books out at any kind of decent pace.

In other words, you need discipline. There will be times that writing your book is fun. You have great ideas and words practically flow off your fingers. And then there are the times you're halfway through a first draft, you hate the story, you hate your characters, and you want to move to the next shiny idea or do something else entirely. You need to keep going at those points, and the main way to do that is to have developed the self-discipline necessary to do it.

My best suggestion here is to work up to it, and make it into a habit. Practice writing at least 15 minutes a day, every day. 15 minutes is much easier to carve out of a busy day than hours and hours. Don't take days off from this. Write more when you have time, but stay consistent on that 15 minutes. Eventually, it does become something of a habit, and you'll find yourself restructuring your time to sneak that in somewhere. At that point, expand if you can, or try two 15 minute periods, or whatever is working for you. Regardless, build it into your schedule, then your habits, and then your mindset. At that point, you have a place to start from.

Lee: This is absolutely the most important thing that separates the professionals from the amateurs. Writing books is a job and needs to be treated as such if you want to be successful at it. Maybe it's a second job, one you do part-time for a few years, but it's still a job. Coders code, teachers teach, and writers write.

Many of the other things you need to do as a published author can be incredibly distracting. Social media is a huge time sink, for which rewards depend greatly upon many factors. Working conventions takes time and energy. Designing promotional materials, running giveaways and other promotions, reading your reviews, editing, handling critiques, examining cover art...all these things will suck your brain right out. Having the discipline to set limits and boundaries and get your butt back in that chair and your fingers back on that keyboard is essential if you intend to publish multiple books.

When you find yourself making excuses for not writing at your usual time more than one day here or there, there are questions you should ask yourself. Are you exhausted because of other things in your life? Do you resent your writing time because you prefer to do X at that time of day? Is something not going right in the story? Is outside stress destroying your concentration or creativity? Do you need more exercise? Figure out the answers and adjust accordingly.

Finish Things

Jeff: There is a certain kind of person I see and talk to at conventions on a regular basis. They approach publishers and authors very excitedly, saying "I'm writing a book!" or "I have an idea for a book!" They want to tell you all about it, with great enthusiasm. Then, the next year, they show up again, very excited. When asked how their book is going, the answers become "I have it saved, because I had an even better idea!" or "It's great! I'm 20,000 words in. That's almost a book, right?"

Other ideas are great. Almost every author I talk to has them. Lots of them. The people who become published authors are the people who can note those ideas down for later, maybe draw a little energy off of the inspiration, and then finish their current project.

And by finishing, let me be clear, I don't just mean the first draft. You need to edit, rewrite, throw away sections of the first work that weren't up to standards, rewrite them, edit some more, find objective people to read and react, make any changes you feel are warranted based on your beta-readers, and re-edit. Then, if the remaining document is somewhere upwards of 55,000 words, you have something like a finished book.

Don't just take my word for it. "Finish" is a piece of advice that's repeated over and over by many successful authors. Once you finish, you're way ahead of a large portion of the writing population.

Lee: Finishing one project is important. Finishing multiple projects is critical. Very few people do well with only one book anymore. Thirty years ago, a publishing contract for one book could provide a decent living for a while. That doesn't happen anymore. Not only do publishers rarely offer major marketing support to new authors these days, but indies almost never land on a bestseller list with their first book, or their second, or even the third or fourth.

If you want to succeed as an author, you need to slide

into a regular writing groove and produce books on some kind of timetable that doesn't stretch across years. To have a chance, you'll want to strive for publishing at least one book and making one or two anthology appearances every year. Even if the anthologies don't have big names or are for charity instead of pay, you're still getting your name out there in places it otherwise wouldn't wind up.

Put Out Your Best Work

Jeff: This would seem to conflict with some of the other advice. I mention what we do, in contrast to the people who treat their book like their baby, and spend years perfecting one story. And again, there's nothing wrong with that if it works for you. But if you want to make a living by writing, you need a stable of work. Yes, a few people will have one of their first books take off and become a bestseller. That's awesome for them. They are also the exceptions, not the rule, and you're much better off planning for the long haul instead of hoping lightning strikes.

So, if the point isn't spending years on each book, then what can you do?

This goes back to treating it like a job. When you shop at a furniture store, you have certain expectations. A craftsman put in the time to get things right. Furniture is expected to hold together through basic transportation and normal use. The wood was cut to precise lengths—fractions of an inch off, and it won't fit together right. However, this doesn't necessarily mean the carpenter carefully selected each piece of wood by hand. It also doesn't mean he smithed every nail himself instead of buying them from a hardware store. He had to finish one job and move onto the next. The store has inventory to fill, and he filled it in a professional manner.

If what he built falls apart or doesn't do what it's supposed to, you won't buy that craftsman's furniture again. He needs to meet a certain standard of quality, balanced against making enough furniture to make a living.

Treat your book and your audience with respect. Write the book, and then treat that first draft like what it is: a first draft. Rewrite it. Then edit for everything obvious. Get help from an editor. Find people to beta read it. Do more rewrites and more edits. Clean it up. Make sure it's readable. Take the time to think it over and fix problems. Have other people read through it and get their feedback. In the end, make sure it's the story you want to tell.

Lee: There are genres in which you can make money and a name for yourself without putting in this kind of effort. If you can publish a first draft rife with typos and poor grammar and feel good about promoting it, more power to you. We don't work that way. Our goal is produce entertainment of quality high enough that anyone would feel comfortable recommending it to those who enjoy that type of story.

It's much easier to proudly promote and sell something of quality than it is to hope people don't notice the problems.

Because they will, and they'll post about them in their reviews. Science fiction readers in particular have very high standards. Those who don't take the time to put out the best book possible may succeed, but they won't have an enduring sort of success.

Judge a Book by its Cover

Jeff: People love to say "Don't judge a book by its cover." But everyone does. And to a degree, they should. Here's why, in my opinion:

1. A good cover should tell people something about the book. What is the author going for. Do they want you to identify with characters? Is this book supposed to be an exciting adventure? Does it have a tone that resonates? Is there a symbol or idea that should stand out?

2. A good cover also tells the reader how much love the author has for their own work. Sloppy or amateurish covers tell people the contents may not be professional either.

When you go for a job interview, you dress to the occasion. Treat your books the same. The cover is your first chance to make an impression on the reader. Make it appropriate to the situation, and make sure the cover gives the very best first impression you possibly can.

Lee: I have a copy of my very first book cover. What I see when I look at it is a snapshot of who I was when I first started this publishing journey: an idiot. I made that cover myself, and it's lousy. I have since upgraded to using professional designers and illustrators, and you can see the difference. They're in the profession because they know more about design and layout than I do.

Never use the cover generators provided by the companies who print or sell books. Although it's possible to create a decent cover with those tools, it's difficult and time-consuming, and you're far more likely to wind up with one that shouts how much of an amateur you are. If you write fantasy and/or science fiction like Jeff and I do, you won't find success with a cover generator. I promise.

There are plenty of affordable options for book covers, including pre-made. Many cover artists who don't routinely get booked up well in advance offer good rates and deals to get their name out there. When looking for a cover artist, don't judge them by their price, judge them by their portfolio.

Craft Quickie Pitches

Lee: You have a book. You have a cover. You have a blurb. All of that will bring a person to your table to look at it. More often than not, this won't sell the book. You still need a nudge to help people figure out if a particular book piques their interest or not. Online, that's what reviews and samples do. Offline, you have to provide that yourself.

The quickie pitch isn't a conversation or an elevator pitch. It's a short, snappy tidbit that offers enough information for a person to judge whether the book sounds like it might be a winner for them. This pitch should highlight what you think is most interesting, unique, unusual, or enticing about the story. It's okay to duplicate parts of the back cover, but don't memorize and regurgitate it.

Examples:

The Fallen: This book features a cranky, sarcastic fortune-teller who hates people. She is, of course, forced to deal with them.

Sound & Fury: Shakespeare Goes Punk: Several authors took Shakespeare plays and reimagined them in various 'punk genres. All the profits from this anthology go directly to a no-kill animal shelter in Lynnwood, Washington.

Girls Can't Be Knights: It features a 16-year-old girl and a 24-year-old man who do *not* have a romance. Instead, they form a proper mentor-apprentice relationship that develops into a father-daughter one.

Dawn of Steam: That's a Regency-style, epistolary story, meaning it's told in letters and journal entries written in the Jane Austen voice. It's non-Victorian steampunk incorporating real historical events.

These examples seem lousy in print. That's because they aren't meant to be read. They're short bursts of interesting information about the books intended to be spoken. The purpose of the quickie pitch isn't to sell the book. It's to entice the customer to want to know more. Once you hit a book they're interested in, lay out your full elevator pitch and have a conversation about it until they either buy the book or walk away.

By the time I started working event tables, I already had seven books across three genres. I needed to be able to whip out a smidge of a pitch for each one. After joining forces with Jeff, we had more than fifteen books across seven genres, and both of us produce them at a rate of at least three per year. We don't have the luxury of expounding on a single book or genre for a full minute. In the span of one minute, we need to be able to match a customer to a book. Quickie pitches help do that job.

Another benefit? They're easy to memorize, for both you and anyone else who might sell your books for you. Memorizing elevator pitches gets tricky when you have five different series. Quickie pitches are significantly easier because they're short and snappy. If you don't have an elevator pitch, when your quickie pitch makes them want to know more, you hand them the book with the blurb side up and a smile.

Jeff: Quickie pitches really do help in terms of getting an idea what a customer is interested in. Just as important is how easy they are for other people to memorize. You're looking at working in a cooperative environment. When working with anyone, listen to their quickie pitch about their books. Memorize it, and then use it the next time you see a customer perusing that book.

Getting Into Conventions

Lee: When you first start looking for conventions to apply to, unless you have vendor friends, you're in for a rude awakening about time and money. Most conventions fill their Dealer Rooms at least six months prior to the convention. Some fill up the day applications open. Some are full the day after the previous convention ends.

Applications for conventions are just that: applications. The fact you want to be in a particular vendor room has little bearing on whether you'll get into it or not. Once you send your application in, which may require an upfront payment of all or part of the vendor fee, the dealer liaison gets to decide if they want you in the room or not.

If you have three or fewer books, you'll probably have better luck getting into the con's Author Alley/Avenue than its vendor room. This is a collection of vendor tables usually placed outside the main vendor room, often lined up in a hallway and specifically designated for authors and small presses only. At larger cons, it may be a subsection of the vendor room. All the suggestions in this book apply equally to dealer rooms and author alleys, as the only real differences are your neighbors, level of security provided, and relative location.

The table fees for conventions, at the time of this writing, range from $50-2500+. Fortunately for you, the higher end fees are for booths much too large to be useful until you have 40+ titles to hawk. Those spaces will normally be appropriate for vendors with high margin goods or names with drawing power. Even big name authors, though, will typically go for mid-range spaces and team up with others to share the costs. Expect to spend $150-250 for a table at a medium or small convention.

Find the Right Partner

Lee: It's easy to find another author who wants to split costs and do events together. If you belong to any writer's groups, associations, or other clumps of people who write, you'll find some. The trick is to find someone where there's mutual benefit to the partnership and matching goals.

I first met Jeff by showing up to an event I'd heard about too late to participate in as an author. I went as an attendee. Eight or nine authors set up with their books, and I talked to each one. I wound up tossing a few books onto my Kindle reading list. One of those books happened to be *Dawn of Steam: First Light*, a novel I decided to take a chance on despite my utter lack of interest in steampunk, the Napoleonic Wars era, airships, or epistolary fiction, because Jeff seemed like a decent guy and took the time to chat with me.

Because I had a good time, I got myself into the next event he organized at the same venue. We chatted, I sold some books, and I found out he needed a ride to Portland for an event. Since I have a car and also wanted to go to that event, and he clearly wasn't a creepy stalker, I offered.

I'm not going to suggest that the *only* way to discover if you can work with someone is to spend two hours in a car with them. However, it works. We chatted the whole way down, then again the whole way back home. Clockwork Dragon would never have happened without those early conversations.

We discovered that we both wanted to do lots of events, publish lots of books, and share costs whenever possible. We also learned we had overlapping geekdom interests.

Looking for a convention partner isn't so different from looking for a life partner, in many ways. The goals and purpose are different, but the need for someone you can communicate and spend time with is essential. You'll be sharing hotel rooms, car trips, and booth time. You might sleep on their couch sometimes and vice versa. Anyone you're going to do that with needs to be someone you *can* do that with.

Jeff: It really does go back to that first event. Lee wasn't the first person, even remotely, to contact me about that event. And I kept coming back with the same response, "This event is full, but I'll be doing more. I would recommend, if you can, showing up for this one, get to know the other authors, and see how these work."

Lee was the only one to do so. So when she not only showed up, talked to everyone, and took notes on that event, but then immediately got back to me expressing interest in the next one, commenting that she'd picked up some of the books, you'd better believe she jumped to the head of the line for that next event.

I knew I'd made the right decision in that next event when, while she was selling her own books, she got someone asking about steampunk and actively walked them over to my table, grabbed a copy of *First Light*, and said "You need to read this."

That drive to Portland was also extremely informative. We determined that we agreed on a lot of our approach to events. We had a similar number of books out, and we both had the same goal at that point: to take what we'd learned in the conventions we'd done so far and figure out how to do better. We saw the value in conventions as a marketing tool, but knew we weren't utilizing them to nearly their maximum potential.

The other really critical thing we discovered: we could not only stand being in the confined space of a small car with each other for 2+ hours, but got to the destination full of energy and ideas. When the trip back produced the same result despite post-event fatigue, I think we both had some idea that we had something good going. We had no idea what it would become as far as business plans, massive road trips, and so on…but knew it was something we could repeat and even wanted to.

That, I think, is particularly big. It's easy to find someone who wants to save money on a convention table. It's a lot harder finding someone with the same drive and professionalism you have. If you're hoping to do quite a few conventions with any kind of consistency at your table, it's very much worth the effort to find those people.

Complementary Skills

Lee: Between Jeff and me, the one skill we share is storytelling. We both write stories, and they happen to be science fiction and fantasy. Aside from that, our skill sets are generally rather different. He has mobility issues; I'm a casual cyclist. He's good with people; I'm good with promotional graphics. And so on.

When it comes to, for example, booth setup and teardown, I do most of the work because I can lift, run, jump, crawl, and otherwise wriggle and move things. Jeff stands back and lets me work, occasionally holding or retrieving things on request, and doing some of the lighter tasks like setting books in stands.

It sounds like I'm getting the short end of the stick until you discover that we got the booth in the first place because he knows Person X who thinks Jeff is awesome. Or maybe Jeff was the one who set up the place we're crashing that night because he knows Person Y with an extra couch and floor space. Or his friends will all be at the con and they'll come by and pick up anything they can afford.

He's brilliant at networking. I'm an energetic workhorse. This is only one example of how we divide responsibilities according to what we're capable of and good at.

If you're both good at all the same things, unless you're somehow both magically good at every single skill needed to run a table, you're going to have a problem. Even if you're both somehow good at everything, the division of labor can easily turn into a ledger or scorecard.

Jeff: This does extend right into the conventions. I like doing panels. I can read comfortably in front of a crowd. I've spent my entire life moving around the country constantly, and having to quickly meet new people. I'm actually not an extrovert, but I can fake it comfortably for periods of time. I also don't at all mind spending a convention behind a table. I love conventions in general, but a lot of the things involved with a convention don't love people with bad knees.

Lee, meanwhile, has a few extremely relevant skills that I lack. She's really, really good at noticing trends. What people notice, what's working or not working, what adjoining tables or authors we're working with are doing well—and she notes it, incorporates the lessons, and brings those things up later.

She also gets the setup duties not only because she's more physically capable—which she is—but because she's simply better at them. She has a sense of table arrangement and visual aesthetics that I lack.

Self-awareness is important at this stage. Determining what your strengths and weaknesses are and trying to find someone who fills in the gaps will help you succeed at conventions.

Taking Breaks

Lee: It's certainly possible to run a table at an event by yourself. Jeff and I both still do from time to time, for one reason or another. When I'm by myself, I miss having someone to crack jokes with. I also miss having someone to rely on when I need a time-out. Working a table is actually work, and regular jobs have to give you breaks for a reason.

If you're by yourself, leaving the table for five minutes can be problematic. Aside from your cashbox, your table is covered in merchandise. Sure, it may be difficult to sell your books, but it's easy to give them away for free. A table full of books and display whatnot is a tempting target for the bibliophile short on cash.

With a partner on hand, you can walk away to have a genuine meal or go to a panel. You can take a stroll around the vendor room and meet people. Should you fall ill, your table will go on.

It's worth noting that working a convention table can be similar to working retail, customer service, or tech support. Customers expect to be deferred to and may not always remember you're a human being, let alone the creator of the work they're looking at. Though it doesn't happen often, I've had people patronize me, hurl sarcasm at me, and tell me they don't read fiction because it's a waste of time. This kind of treatment—especially when you both know they could have walked past in silence instead—can be upsetting and frustrating. With a partner on hand, not only can they sympathize with you, they can also give you time to go decompress in private.

Jeff: The part I focus on the most in the above is "working a table is actually work." Most of your friends won't get that. They're using their vacation time or fun money to attend the event. They want to do parties and panels and hang out. As a vendor, you can't do that. That's not to say cons aren't fun—they definitely are, or can be. But when you're there to make a part of your living, it's a whole different thing. It's really nice to have someone to talk to who gets that.

Part of the work is the dead time. Sitting at a table by yourself when there's no customers around is both frustrating and boring. Having someone to help pass the time in those cases can really improve the convention experience.

This is important not only for the sake of boredom, but because if you look bored at the table during the slow times, when potential customers do see you, they're much less likely to engage. They may well see you before you see them, so it's important that someone at the table is looking alert, and like they want to be there.

And then, of course, there's bathroom breaks. Without someone to watch your booth, you can't even reliably step away for those short periods. That can make a convention miserable in a hurry.

One of the things I bring to the table is a generally pretty consistent demeanor and a lot of patience in most circumstances. In any position dealing with the public, there's always a chance of stress and frustration, and I'm not immune —but I have a pretty high tolerance in most cases. I'll do my ranting and unloading about things on the drive home, quite often as part of a back and forth. Unless I'm doing a panel or some other planned event, I don't feel the need to leave the table very often. Lee knows this about me, and generally doesn't hesitate to just let me know she's going to wander for ten minutes.

The upside to some of this for the person with bad knees and a cane who can't get up and wander often—when she does take a break, she'll often check and see if I want a refill on water or the like. That's a lot more worthwhile to me in terms of surviving a con comfortably than time away from the table, and it certainly saves my knees during those long conventions.

Someone Who Can Sell Your Books

Jeff: Lee reads my work. I read Lee's work. We knew early on that each of us had skills the other didn't. We both knew we had similar levels of drive and similar long-term goals. What really turned this into a partnership effort, in my opinion, was when we proved we could and would sell each other's books.

At a convention with the two of us, one of the things you'll hear over and over is "I've read that one. It's a really good book." Or even "I haven't gotten to that one yet, but here's what readers have said." And this is important. Having someone who is not the author saying that a book is good is more meaningful than all the advertisement in the world. It does help, and it does sell books.

Aside from simply knowing the level of preparation and what to expect, this is one of the biggest differences between working with Lee and working with random authors.

In a dramatic example, I worked with one author who usually sells well. I hadn't worked with him directly before, but we knew each other from working the same events at different tables. He wanted someone to go in on an expensive table at a huge event. Because there was no doubt the audience was there, and others who'd vended at that event had good things to say, I went for it.

He was, as it turns out, certainly professional in a lot of ways, but he was very focused on his own books. He had a hard-sell, my-pitch-first approach. If I didn't start talking fast enough, I'd never get a word in at all. I couldn't reliably take breaks, because no one would be making an effort to sell my stuff.

In all, the show was terrible for both of us. We didn't meet our costs, and it wasn't a positive experience. The thing is, the audience was there. I think it could have been a much better show with the right cooperative approach. I was pushed into a mode where I wasn't comfortable on my end, and meanwhile, he wasn't taking advantage of the variety on the table to match customers with books. I plan to give that show another try, this time with Lee, to see if we can do better.

Lee: In my opinion, the biggest bonus of selling someone else's work is the significantly reduced pressure. I suffer from a delightful mix of mild social anxieties that make initial overtures daunting. Deducing social cues to know when to let a person read the back cover and when to plow ahead with pitching takes effort and practice. The opportunity to not have the added weight of my own financial well-being on top of any conversation is welcome.

I want Jeff to succeed, and I want his books to sell, but if this particular person doesn't buy the copy of *First Light* they're reading the back of, it's impossible to construe that as a rejection of me or my work. Conversely, when they do decide to buy it, that's a win. Why is it a win? If one of us doesn't sell any books, that person will have to stop going to conventions and events. Having to do all this stuff by myself would suck, and I wouldn't be able to afford to go to as many of them.

As a general rule, Jeff and I tend to sell each other's books at least as often as we sell our own. I'm always happy to point out the steampunk for those asking about it, a genre I don't write in. He's happy to direct people to my superheroes or snark fantasy, both genres he has no books in. Because we each do this, I have zero worries about wandering off to take in a panel or survey the rest of the vendor room. Likewise, Jeff knows he can go sit on a panel and I'll talk up his books as much as I do my own.

In fact, there have been a few events where I practically ignored my own books in favor of selling his simply because I didn't feel up to the onerous challenge of sticking my books in strangers' hands and talking them up.

Jeff: This is a centerpiece of making conventions or other sales events work as part of a group. Everyone needs to be able to at least give the quickie pitch about any book on the table, and have a willingness to do so. Everyone wants their own books to sell, obviously. Everyone benefits from having a greater breadth of books on the table. Plus, if you prove that you'll sell someone else's books, they may be more willing to return the favor.

If they don't, you may not be working with the right people.

Finding the right people and getting that approach down is essential for a few critical things to your long-term success at a convention:

1. Everyone involved needs to sell books to see the value in conventions. If one person makes a lot of money but no one else sells, they're unlikely to want to keep doing conventions.

2. The table as a whole ultimately needs to make its costs back. Any one person's stuff alone is unlikely to do this, at least regularly. Conventions are an investment, and one you eventually want to see some return on.

3. At conventions, customers often come in waves. Having 2-3 workers means your table can handle multiple customers at once with no one coming off as rude by interrupting one conversation to start another. At these times, you don't want to risk losing a sale for the table because of an inconsistent approach. The person you're talking to might be more interested in someone else's book, but what about the people you're not talking to?

4. Few people buy and read just one book. Catch someone's

interest, provide them a good experience, and show a genuine want to match their tastes instead of yours. You'll be surprised how many people leave the table with 3 or 4 books, which may include yours.

5. Happy customers come back. Create a comfortable environment, give people a good customer service experience, and make people happy with what you've given them, and they will return to your table at later conventions. People return to the same conventions year after year. The new customers available at each convention are limited. You always need to be trying to reach new customers, but creating loyal fans of your brand helps you just as much.

Lee: We've both had the experience of working in a group where one person just doesn't get this. That one person refuses to step back and let people approach at their own pace, insists upon shoving their book under noses, and/or pushes until the customer either buys or flees. Or both. If they buy, it's a low-value pressure sale, and if they don't, it's a loss for the entire group.

That person doesn't get invited back. They may try to go it alone, and they may do well for a while, but eventually, people will avoid them. Don't be that person.

My Favorite Sale

Jeff: My very favorite sale from this year was at Worldcon in Spokane:

Customer picks up Lee's *Dragons in Pieces.*

Me: I've read that one. It's a great book. I'm looking forward to reading book two.

Customer: *Looks at me suspiciously* Are you the author?

Me: Oh no, the author is over there. I work with her all the time.

Customer: If you two work together all the time, how do I know you're not just trying to push her work on me?

Me: If I didn't believe in her work, and think it was good, we wouldn't work together all the time.

Customer: Sold.

The approach obviously worked in that case. I think what's more important is that it remains my favorite and most memorable sale of the year. I've sold hundreds of my own books at conventions. I didn't personally make a penny off of this sale. He bought only the one book. But it was the one he was interested in. I proved that matching a customer to a book and helping the strength of the table partnership was more important than pushing my stuff. That increases the chances Lee is going to want to keep working with me, gives her tangible motivation to return the favor, allows her to feel comfortable walking around or taking breaks, and strengthens the table and the brand as a whole.

Display Kit

Lee: You have books, you have a partner, and you've signed up for a convention. Now you need gear.

Jeff: Don't just pack for a convention the night before and expect to be ready. Either keep your show kit mostly packed and restock after each show, or pack up early in the week. This way you know how many books you have of each title, their condition, if anything is missing, etc. Give yourself some time to deal with any unexpected problems before you leave for the con. For most of us, the convention days themselves can be stressful enough without adding any extra problems right beforehand.

Lee: The first, most important piece of gear you need is something to cart the rest of your gear inside. I've tried several options and am happiest with a hard-sided, wheeled suitcase. I recommend using one with four swivel-mounted wheels. While the two-wheel varieties may come with larger wheels better capable of surmounting obstacles, they're less versatile. I've been in situations where I managed everything in one trip because I could push the suitcase in front of me like a cart.

Anything packed inside a soft-sided case or bag will eventually result in damage, either to the contents or to you as you carry it. Insulating material takes up far too much space to make such containers attractive.

The next best option for gear transport is a hard plastic container. As the least attractive option, you can use a cardboard box. The biggest problem with cardboard boxes is their lack of durability. Rain, snow, errant toddlers, your lunch…anything can ruin cardboard.

The next most important piece of gear is a wheeled cart or a dolly. Use this to carry your books and anything that doesn't fit in your display case. Having used both, I prefer a wheeled cart. It's easier on me, my back, and my temper. Folding carts that store and pack relatively well are reasonably priced and generally decent quality.

Beyond those two critical pieces of gear, you'll need the display items themselves. The lists below are divided into the Essential gear I use at every show, the Helpful gear I use often but may not need every time, and the gear that's Contingent upon certain situations.

Essential

Book holders: Most authors use some type of picture or dish display as book holders. There are few wrong choices. Pick something that suits your style and genre, or something generic that's easy to pack. Whatever you choose, though, do not use hinge-style dish holders. More often than not, this type of holder will fall over anytime someone touches the book.

Essential
Book holders
Tablecloth
Safety pins
Pens
Credit card reader
Change for cash customers
Price stickers or price sheet with display method
Water bottle
Clipboard
Newsletter signup sheet
Business cards

Tablecloth: Most of the time, you'll need a 6-foot trade show tablecloth. This is the kind with all four sides hanging down so you can stuff your book boxes underneath and no one has to see your legs, lunch, boxes, or garbage. Some shows offer 8 foot tables, so it may be worthwhile to also have an 8-foot tablecloth. Often, a show can provide one, but you never know what color(s) you'll get, whether it'll hang to the floor, or if you'll be charged for it. The best bet is to have your own in a color you want.

Safety pins: If you get a banner with grommets or hangers, safety pins are an excellent way to attach it to the front of your table. When your tablecloth is too big for the table, you pin it up so no one trips over it. Pin a plastic bag to your tablecloth in the back for lightweight garbage. And so on. There are so many helpful uses for safety pins, it's smart to have at least one package of them.

Pens: As an author, you need things to sign your books. Always bring at least two pens in case one decides not to work. Keep one or two in your pocket and you'll never be without. I keep at least five in my display case at all times.

Jeff:
Pens disappear at conventions. At least, my pens disappear. I brought a dozen to a convention. Three shows later, I had to borrow a pen from Lee. Bring them and keep better track of them than I do.

Credit card reader: Clockwork Dragon uses Square to accept credit cards, calculate and manage sales tax, and track inventory. Their online software also includes reports that facilitate the group using one account for all our sales and easily calculating the amount to pay each member. Square's card readers connect to a smartphone or tablet via audio jack or Bluetooth. Keep this reader in your display case so you never forget it. There are other options, but we recommend

Square for ease of use and excellence of tools.

<u>Cash change:</u> Deciding how much cash change you need is tricky for any small business. Generally, you want to have enough change to facilitate at least five customers using a $20 bill and purchasing only one of your books.

<u>Price sheet/stickers</u>: Your books need to declare their prices. If they're all the same price, your life is easy. You can make up a small sign and set it on the table. If you carry books at different prices, you'll either need a price sheet or stickers. If you have more than five books at more than one price, I recommend one inch round stickers, which can be printed or written on.

Jeff:
<u>Water bottle:</u> I'm going to emphasize the 'water bottle' bit here, though with a slight caveat. You should definitely stay hydrated. You may also want to consider caffeinated, or otherwise get some help staying awake for the long, dead stretches.

I don't use a water bottle. I drink carbonated water instead. Hydration, plus I do a ton of talking at conventions, and the carbonation helps my throat a lot more than normal water. That's specific to me, though. Figure out what works for you—but start with a water bottle, and make sure, in some fashion, you keep water on hand.

<u>Clipboard:</u> The clipboard is for holding your newsletter signup

sheet. Make sure you keep one pen with the signup sheet. This doesn't need to be placed prominently, though that's ideal. Once you get past ten books, you may not have space for it. Keep it behind the display if you need to and offer it to people when you make a sale or sense genuine interest.

Business cards: I like business cards because they're small. Small things take up very little table space. They're also relatively cheap. Clockwork Dragon uses a business card with our logo, motto, and website on the front, and our names and website QR code on the back. It doubles nicely as a bookmark and has a bit of white space for jotting down notes. We hand them out to anyone who might be interested in looking us up later or prefers ebooks over paper. We also tuck one inside every book.

Helpful

Half of the Helpful list consists of the things you need when disaster strikes. Something rips? Duct tape. Something won't stay but duct tape will ruin it? Cloth tape. Something needs to be stuck together? Rubber bands, scotch tape, or zip ties. Something needs to be unstuck? Scissors. I recommend against a knife, as that can invite Security issues.

Cash box: A cash box is nice to have because it can lock. On the downside, they're usually large enough to not fit into a backpack, so it's obvious what you're carrying. I like having one because it looks semi-professional compared to keeping change in your wallet or pocket, and it's better than leaving cash lying around. If you carry coin change, a cash box is essential. If you don't, it's just a nice thing to have.

Bookmarks and other swag: Many authors swear by bookmarks, stickers, keychains, buttons, postcards, badge ribbons, and other swag items. Different swag is popular at different conventions. Pick whichever two or three things fit within your budget, you're willing to wear/use yourself, and look good with your cover or promotional art. Bookmarks are typically a no-brainer for people who read physical books. When you have a lot of books, keep the different designs down to three at most.

Helpful
Duct tape
Scotch tape
Zip ties
Rubber bands
Cloth tape
Scissors
Cash box
Bookmarks
Other swag
Blank paper
Bedsheet or flat tablecloth

Blank paper: Always good to have for a variety of reasons, not the least of which is jotting down notes about the new series you just thought of during a lull. Keep a few sheets on hand, and you can make up a quick sign to preemptively answer a question you keep getting asked, let people know you'll be back in five minutes, make an impromptu nameplate for a panel, or create signage for a new set deal on the fly.

Bedsheet or flat tablecloth: Use this to cover your table after hours. It's not a lock and key, but most people considering swiping something won't bother when they can't see what they're taking or have to do something as obvious to potential onlookers as lift a sheet.

Contingent

Contingent
Table
Swag holder
Shopping bags
Gallon plastic freezer bags
Standing mat
Book rack
Riser(s)
Backdrop

Table: Most conventions will provide one table at no additional cost. Some will not. Most local fairs and festivals will not provide tables, even for a fee. If you intend to work a lot of events, it's worthwhile to invest in a folding 6-foot trade show table. As you publish more books, you may also want an 8-foot and a 4-foot table, depending upon how you choose to set up your display. A 10x10-foot space can be filled nicely with one 6-foot and one perpendicular 4-foot table, or one 6 and one 8 for a corner.

Swag holder: Business cards and bookmarks look fine stacked or fanned on a table. They may look better in a holder that takes up less space. We sometimes use a combination tray that holds one stack of business cards, two stacks of bookmarks, and one or two stacks of postcards. Other times, we use a dragon head on a plate holding business cards in its mouth. Which props we use for this purpose depends on the amount of space we have. Other types of swag may be best collected in a basket or small bowl to keep them from falling all over the place.

Shopping bags: Many conventions give out swag bags, making shopping bags unnecessary. Fairs and festivals rarely give out such things, but people often bring their own in expectation of purchasing. Book buyers don't tend to want shopping bags unless you're their first stop and they get several books at once. As a result, you can easily get through any given event, including large ones, with 10 bags. Don't get the cheap plastic ones that hold only one book unless you only want to sell one book to any given customer. Bags can be branded with your name—only do so if it seems cost effective to you.

Gallon plastic freezer bags: When you work an outdoor event, it's advisable to add one-gallon freezer bags to your show kit. Bring at least one per title. Seal a book inside and it's protected from the weather. Customers will understand that you don't want lots of books on your table in the rain and won't be put off by the rest of the books being safely tucked away in plastic containers.

Standing mat: Although I regard my standing mat as essential, it won't fit at every convention. Mine is a 3/4 inch retail mat, and I love it for long days at cons. Unfortunately, some cons just don't have enough space behind the table for this to be feasible with two people and banners and a garbage bag and books in boxes and on and on. It's most important when the floor is bare concrete. When there's carpet, it matters much less.

Book rack: Even if you only have three books, you may want to consider some kind of rack to display them instead of individual holders. Once you have a number of books, a few bits of merchandise, and some clever display props, your books may not all fit on the table without using some kind of rack or shelf. Search until you find a rack that suits you and the type of display you set up.

Risers: These are what they sound like: things to raise your books. Multi-leveled displays look nicer than single-level ones. This can be anything from a cardboard box under your tablecloth to a tabletop bookshelf to a plastic box with a fancy bit of cloth draped over it. A word of warning: some conventions do not allow cardboard boxes to be used as part of a display for fire code reasons. They probably won't notice the one under your bright blue cloth, but it's best not to take the chance.

Backdrop: Having one looks nice and provides extra branding or promo opportunities, but it's entirely optional. They take up space in your car and generally require assembly and disassembly. The longer your setup and teardown, the earlier you have to show up and the later you leave. We sometimes use a backdrop. It depends on two main things: space and length of show. If there's no space, we don't use it. Likewise, spending the time and effort to put it up isn't worth it for a three-hour reading event.

Our backdrop is a 5-foot-wide black panel, and we hang a secondary brand banner plus a banner with our photographs and names on it. When possible, we also hang a promo banner on it. That particular width is a good fit for us in a 10-foot booth because we can set standing banners on either side of it and not worry about the space. In a smaller booth, we can still use it to provide a visual barrier between our space and the space behind us, but we usually opt for the standing banners to fulfill that role instead. They're lighter in weight, take up less space, and set up much faster.

Name Tags

Lee: Something few people think of for convention gear is a name tag. Cons give you a badge, and it usually has your name on it. Why would you need a name tag?

The purpose of a convention badge is to make it clear you belong there. At a glance, the staff and volunteers need to know if you should have access to this room at this time. From the convention's point of view, your name is the least important piece of information on your badge. Accordingly, it's printed small or in a font that's not terribly easy to read at a glance. Additionally, a lot of badges have only one point of contact with a lanyard, causing them to twist all the time. If you collect ribbons and buttons, which you should do if it appeals to you, that's also distracting from your name.

When a person walks up to your table, they don't know who you are. You *want* them to know who you are. Your con badge won't solve this problem.

Whether you're getting a durable name tag or a temporary one with a special show logo, include the word "Author." Own your identity and profession. Wear both proudly.

Books

Lee: The one question I had when I first started doing events was, "How many books do I bring?" Seasoned pros and fellow newbies alike had a hard time providing a real answer that I could use for the specific events on my calendar. No one knows how many of book X will sell at any given event, not even the pros who've been doing it for thirty years. We all have to make a best guess.

In my experience, it's better to have too many books than not enough. If you run out of books, that means you're done. Some conventions will punish you for that by assessing a fee for taking up space with no product. Many get snippy if you pack up early. Without books, you can hand out bookmarks and cards, but those probably won't get you much in return, as people want to see genuine books on your table.

Having too many left over is a problem of a different sort. If you need to ship them home, you have to pay for that. Shipping books from one convention to another may also cost you sales tax or other stupid fees. Piling everything back into your car is, of course, work.

For any convention, regardless of size, it's unlikely that an unknown, self-published or small press author will sell more than 20 copies of any given title. If you have only one title at a big convention, people will steer away from you because there's no guarantee you'll produce more from their point of view. If you have multiple titles, your sales will be spread out among them.

Until you have a solid fan base of thousands, or a sizable fan base in the city of the convention, the first book of any series will always sell more than subsequent books in that series. The first and second time you go to any particular convention, you can certainly count on selling your Book 1 titles over Book 2+.

The advice I did manage to collect does have some value. Professionals suggested I bring enough books to make back the cost of the table, plus a few extra. That's the rule of thumb I go by, except I never can tell which books will be a hit at any given convention. Sometimes, one book surprises me by selling more than usual and another one by not selling at all.

Generally, I suggest 10 copies of first books and standalones for small conventions and 15 for large ones, plus 4 and 6 respectively for second books and beyond. At a con where some title seems like it resonates with the themes of the con, bring 20 of that title. For anthologies, unless it's for a charity, 5 is sufficient for most events, regardless of size. Charity anthologies, especially for well-known and universally liked/loved organizations, tend to do better, so bring the same number as a Book 1.

If you're offering set deals, bump the number of included book 2+ by a few copies, to as many as 7 (smaller cons) and 10 (larger cons).

Note: if you want to do decorative stacking, bring at least 15 copies of each book you wish to stack. Depending upon the thickness of the book(s) in question and how you decide to stack them, you may need as many as 30.

After several events, you'll see what does well and what doesn't, and be able to adjust your personal numbers accordingly.

Jeff: Even if these numbers seem high, they're good guidelines. When starting out, you want to fill the space and make your table look full. You paid for the whole table: use it. As weird as it sounds, it helps you to look like you expect to be successful. I don't know how much of this is psychological, and if a fair amount of it is, if it's the psychology of the seller or the buyer. Whatever it is, we have noticed a positive difference when we make sure things are laid out such that it appears we have plenty of inventory.

Plan for Damage

Jeff: The very first time I went to Orycon in Portland, I took the bus. It got me there on time, but in the process, my bags were put into the baggage storage area. Half of my books were damaged due to getting wet, and in addition to the cost of lost books, I had no way to restock that weekend.

The first time I did Maple Valley Days, we had a tent, so I thought I was safe from the rain. It turned out that water still collected and seeped through in a couple of dripping spots at one edge. A few more books were ruined.

There was also the incident where someone brought chocolate as a table interest piece. It sort of worked, except very few people who came over for fancy chocolates actually bought books. What did happen was we got a bunch of kids who handled chocolate, then handled books.

No matter what, things will happen. Books are fairly fragile items in a lot of ways, and a little water or sticky candy can ruin one, at least in terms of being able to sell it. Sometimes, there's nothing you can do but hope you have enough stock to make up for it and last out the show. But keep in mind what you're selling, be aware of the environment, and protect appropriately.

Arrange the Environment

Lee: Setting up a convention table is an art form, not a science. Your goal is to create an inviting display that showcases your work. As you publish more books, your display will evolve to include the new releases. It's otherwise not unlike a book cover in many respects. Use your table to make yourself look professional, invested in the books you've written, open to conversation, and prepared for the most likely scenarios.

That seems like a tall order. Start with the obvious: your books. Place one copy of each book on the table to start with. Arrange series in order from left to right or front to back. Otherwise arrange books based upon sub-genre. Most customers are more comfortable with all the steampunk books together rather than having them scattered across the table and tucked between fantasy novels, and it's easier to point to that part of the table and say, "That's our steampunk section."

Once you have your books arranged, add more copies of each book, keeping the stacks roughly even. Make sure your stacks aren't taller than you while sitting so passersby know someone is there.

There are two basic methods of book display: decorative stacking and using stands. The two methods can be used independently or combined. Both are attractive, both have downsides.

Decorative stacking involves tilting or rotating stacked

books to form a spiral, pyramid, or other interesting shape. This generally requires a large number of books to look good. If you happen to have thirty copies of a book, try this method. It looks nice and draws the eye. It's also incredibly easy to mess up by touching it or the table.

Examples of Decorative Stacking

Using stands means you prop one copy of the book on a stand of some sort so the cover is tilted to appeal to a person standing on the other side of your table. You can use a stand directly on the table or on top of a stack of books. This offers an obvious copy for a reader to pick up and examine. The most important downside of this? It requires gear, and gear costs money and has to be schlepped.

In addition to your books and swag, you'll want banners or posters of some kind. Unless you have three or fewer books, these probably won't go on the table, but rather in front of it or behind you. Whatever you use for these, make sure they evoke you, your books, and/or your genre(s). Like book covers, they should be as professional as you can afford and should match the content of what you're selling. Fortunately, art for these tends to be cheaper because it's not for commercial use, and you can usually use your already acquired book covers on them.

Do not put anything on your table that you don't want to clean up later. Glitter and confetti are a pain. Other small ornaments can be annoying and time-consuming to deal with, and easily lost. Don't be the vendor the con staff has to clean up after, because they'll remember when you submit for a table next year.

Some cons specifically prohibit stickers, and others may only frown on them. Be aware that any stickers with identifying information on them may cause you trouble later if con or site staff find them stuck to floors, walls, bathroom stalls, or anywhere else. Badge ribbons are usually exempt from this.

Catch the Eye

Jeff: Your goal is to make people stop. At conventions, people tend to sweep through the dealer room. Sometimes they have a destination in mind, sometimes they only stop for something really eye-catching.

Some vendors get people to stop through the hard-sell approach. They push books at people, shout at people as they go past, and so on. We advise very strongly against that approach. Don't become the used car salesman of convention floors.

So, if you're not going to actively go block people or shout at them, how do you do it? Start by dressing suitably for the occasion and drawing attention yourself. Lee and I each have our regular con-wear, which includes fancy hats that tend to draw a lot of attention. That's a start. Taking the time to make your booth visually appealing and eye-catching will help you even more. This is where banners, table signs, visible advertising for special details, and putting your prettiest book covers out visible all come in.

Above all, you want to make the space something that customers want to come into—it's already assumed you want them to come into it. Focus on increasing the appeal to your customer, not on badgering them.

Professional Displays

Jeff: This is one where Lee is the master. She handles a lot of the table setup and arrangement for just this reason. At shows I do by myself, though, I certainly try to incorporate the ideas. Just like you want to dress professionally to make an impression when going to a job interview, your booth needs to pass inspection by the con-goers you're hoping will stop.

This is always a tricky process, since you frequently need to adjust on the fly, based on the space you have, the distance to the wall, and room on the table itself. Regardless, this is where things like banners, backdrops, and table interest pieces help you—as long as you aim them at the audience and don't overdo it.

Right now, some example items we have that see a lot of use, with no other purpose beyond being decoration: we have a table-front banner, and another we can hang on the front of a tent or on the back of a booth space. Each of us have individual banners showing off our most notable series. We've got action figures, 3D-printed dragons, and other small pieces. We also have a video display up at our table at most shows. Of course, there's always the trick of balancing display items and books.

Lee: There are two keys to a good, professional display. Each is equally important and essential: first-hand experience and practice. No one creates a stunning booth display on the spot and in a vacuum.

Step 1: Go to a convention and walk around the vendor's room. See what catches your eye. Watch other attendees and see where they cluster. Pay attention to the booths of both big names and small. Note the differences and similarities. Take pictures. Examine them later.

Step 2: Put all your stuff out at home and arrange it. Move things around until you think it looks good, then get a second and third opinion. Take pictures. Examine them side-by-side with the pictures from step one.

How to cheat at this: Gather everything you want to display, go to your first con, and set it up so all the books are visible and you have some swag laid out. Accept it's not perfect and spend the rest of the setup time strolling around the room, checking out other displays. Adapt your display to match the ones that appeal to you, using whatever you have on hand. Take a walk during the con or after the room closes for the evening. Adapt again. Make notes for next time.

Cheating isn't a bad option, to an extent. When I did my first event by myself, I'd followed Steps 1 and 2. When Jeff and I worked together for the first time, I didn't have Jeff's books before the show to mock up a display. We had to arrange on the fly and some things I'd used by myself wouldn't fit. However, you still have to have items on hand to adapt your display. If all you have are books, swag, and hope, there's not much to work with.

As an added wrinkle, the space you get may not be what you're expecting. Sometimes, a 6-foot table has 6 feet behind it. Sometimes, it has 3 feet. Sometimes when you get a booth, you get a corner. Sometimes, you wind up sandwiched between two costume vendors with eight-foot-tall racks holding merchandise that swings into your space. Sometimes, what they call "6 feet" is really more like 4 or 5 because you have to be able to get around the table.

When you have less than four books to display, fill up the rest of the table with art, swag, and decoration. As you release more books, you'll have less and less use for decorative whatnot because you'll need more and more space for books. Keep that in mind when deciding what to purchase or make for your table.

Keep your displays relevant to your books and your brand. If your books don't feature dragons, don't put any dragon art on the table. If you write only adult fiction, don't set out display items that only appeal to kids. Your goal isn't to attract everyone. It's to attract people who would be a good fit for your books. Use character art from your books, blown-up copies of your best covers, and other bits and bobs that relate to your genre and sub-genre(s).

Holiday-themed displays can work. They can also be a monumental waste of money and space. If you're working a Halloween show, feel free to put out a little battery-powered jack-o-lantern, but don't bring a big one unless you're selling a Halloween themed book involving a jack-o-lantern. Likewise for Christmas, or any other holiday decorations. Bring a little something to fill in the small holes if you want, but otherwise stick with what's relevant to you.

Zen and the Art of Book Arrangement

Lee: The single most important thing to remember about arranging books: your ego is more of a hindrance than a help. Obviously, everyone wants their own book to be front and center and pitched and hyped as much as possible. This is fine if you're the only one working the table. It's not so great if you're working with a partner or a group.

If you want to sell books, the ones in the center front need to be the ones that will draw people in. Once a person is drawn in, they'll look at everything else, and there will be chances to pitch other books. They still have to walk up in the first place.

For events and conventions that last more than one day, we like to rearrange the books each day. Swapping two books or series can make a dramatic difference in the look of the table, and people who didn't stop on the previous day may think they missed your table the first time. Additionally, if something you didn't expect is doing well, move it to the front.

If you have a book on your table generating zero interest, you'll have to make a decision about it. That book may not be a good fit for the audience, or it may need to spend some time in the spotlight.

When you have a book that the audience has no interest in, you might as well move it to the back or off to the side. We've been to conventions where the majority of people wanted something specific, as if they'd all had a conference and swore a blood oath to only seek out hard science fiction. In this case, there's nothing you can do to make people want epic fantasy.

On the other hand, the lack of interest may be a reason to move it front and center. If it has a good cover, a good title, and is a good book, and people seem interested in or open to the genre, rotate it into a preferred position and see what happens.

Jeff: Additionally, watch customers as they come in. Watch for what first grabs their attention. The things front and center are important, but sometimes, if everyone is coming in from one direction, the first thing on a corner, or the first elevated display will grab a lot of attention. Shift things around between days based on this information, and use your strongest selling points to make the best possible first impression.

As Lee noted, your ego is only going to hurt you here. Be objective in terms of "best." If you have a title or pretty cover, or whatever, that is a proven seller at multiple shows, position it to take best advantage.

Killer Titles

Jeff: Sechin Tower is one of the most important pillars of Clockwork Dragon, and he barely comes to any events. He has a busy life that prevents him from attending many conventions, and that's okay. Lee and I have read his books, we believe in them, and we can sell them. We also consider him to provide a lot of value to the table, and one of the biggest reasons is *The Non-Zombie Apocalypse.*

People see that title, and they stop. They might buy it, they might not, but regardless, they stop. They then browse other books that didn't grab their attention on the first pass. I'm amazed at the amount of times people who buy Sechin's books leave with 2 or 3 or 5 others. His work achieves one of the first big goals we've gone into: making people stop. It also sells other books.

Lee: Of all my books, *Girls Can't Be Knights* is the first one I set out on a table that made people—mostly women—march up to talk to me. The conversation usually starts like this:

Them, indignantly: Girls can too be knights!
Me: Yes, that's the point of the book.

Although they don't always proceed from this point to making a purchase, approximately 95% of those who approach the table because they saw that title do pick it up, read the back cover, and listen while I pitch it. Many of them wind up buying something—either this book or another one—or taking a bookmark for someone they know. This is a title that makes people stop, with a supporting cover that lets it do that job. Goal!

Jeff: The charity anthologies I help head up serve a lot of the same purpose. *Sound & Fury: Shakespeare Goes Punk* doesn't make me a dime. All the profits go to PAWS Animal Rescue. But it's worth it for me to bring to conventions not only because I support the charity with a passion, but because, man, do people stop when they read the title. Sometimes they move on, sometimes they look at other things too, sometimes they grab the one book. All of those are fine. We've made an impression, and hit our first goal. People looking over that book also give me the opportunity to say, "That one is for charity," which tends to be a really fantastic selling point.

Lee: Having multiple books on a table with this quality gives us an edge, and they're best placed either front and center or on a jutting-out corner. The hard part? It's tricky to know what will do this. Sometimes, a title seems really arresting in your head, and even to your friends, but no one else stops for it. Most often, it's the title you think is kinda cool but not particularly noteworthy. When I came up with "Girls Can't Be Knights," it was a statement several characters make in the book, and I had no idea it would provoke such a strident reaction from so many people.

Jeff: A lot of the best results really are accidental. Authors put a lot of time into coming up with their titles, and you never know what's going to provoke a reaction. Lee's *Girls Can't Be Knights* was one of those really happy accidents. When you do find these books, put them in a prominent spot on the table and make absolutely sure the title is visible, even if it's not yours.

I'll keep stressing—because it really is that important—your first mission is getting people to stop without being too pushy about it. You want them to stop entirely of their own volition.

Striking Covers

Jeff: At the risk of sounding like a broken record, great, eye-catching covers make people stop. Sometimes they get the book that grabbed them, sometimes they get something else, and sometimes they look and move on—but having a few really eye-grabbing covers at a table really helps the overall success of the table.

Foul is Fair has an amazing cover for this. It's bright and colorful, highly detailed, has strange elements—butterflies and a sword—mixed together, and the colors stand out against the books we tend to surround it with.

The Dawn of Steam series is a weirder case. They aren't bright and they don't stand out from a distance. However, they *are* very detailed, high quality art. Each of the three books is a different color, but they still evoke each other, and speak volumes about what sort of books they are. People may not stop for them in quick walk-bys, but once people do stop, having some high quality artwork on the table helps create a positive impression, and helps sell the other books, even if the Dawn of Steam novels aren't really what they're looking for.

Book Pricing

Lee: Setting prices for conventions is one part math, one part psychology, and one part practicality. Online, people are enticed by the magic of .99 on the end of a price. In person, people prefer an even, round number. Stick within two dollars of the price you sell online.

Good price points for paperback books range from $5-25. The thicker the book, the more people are willing to pay for it. Books between about 30k-120k words can safely be priced $10-15 without causing the majority of customers to balk. If the book is too thin to have words on the spine, stay at or below $10. Nonfiction books and illustrated books can be priced up to $5 higher than fiction books. Remember, you're not a big name, so you can't demand premium prices. Charge enough to show the book is worth something, but not so much it looks like you're price-gouging.

Although it incurs extra paperwork on your end, and reduces the amount you make per book, we strongly recommend including sales tax in your cash prices. Coins are a hassle. No one likes carrying pennies around, and most people are fine paying an extra dollar to have sales tax included.

Using Square gives you three options for how to handle sales tax. You can charge it on top of every price, which requires carrying coin change around. You can have Square calculate the tax as included in every price, which facilitates bookkeeping on your end while allowing you to use whole dollar prices.

The third option is to charge sales tax on credit sales, but include it in the cash price. At the time of writing, Square offers "Dining Options" which can be used to create a "Tax Rule" that disables sales tax for an order. This does require you to figure out how much tax you need to pay on the cash sales, which is a bookkeeping issue you'll have to stay on top of. The upside is it charges the extra tax amount to the customers who cause you to incur a card processing fee while still letting you avoid coin change.

Set Deals

Jeff: All of the credit goes to Roslyn McFarland for this one. We might have thought about it eventually, but we didn't have to. This was one of those cases where we saw something that worked, it fit in with our Soft Sell approach, and it was really easy to incorporate. That's a great combination. It's worked out nicely for us, and Roslyn has been happy to be credited for the idea.

This is simple: people like to feel like they're getting a deal. Most people prefer to get the first book in a series, to give it a try. We've discovered, though, if you offer a discount for the set and you make that deal visible on the table, you vastly increase your set sales. The small loss is well worth it for actually moving the books.

We use small placards with the name of the set, and the

individual and set prices. Even if it's just $5 off of a 3 book set, it really does help.

Lee: Simple pop-up placards for these deals can be made very cheaply. Normal printer paper can be folded into fourths and taped together in a triangle shape. Print the information on either of the middle fourths, not the ends. Fancier ones can be printed on cardstock or blank greeting cards.

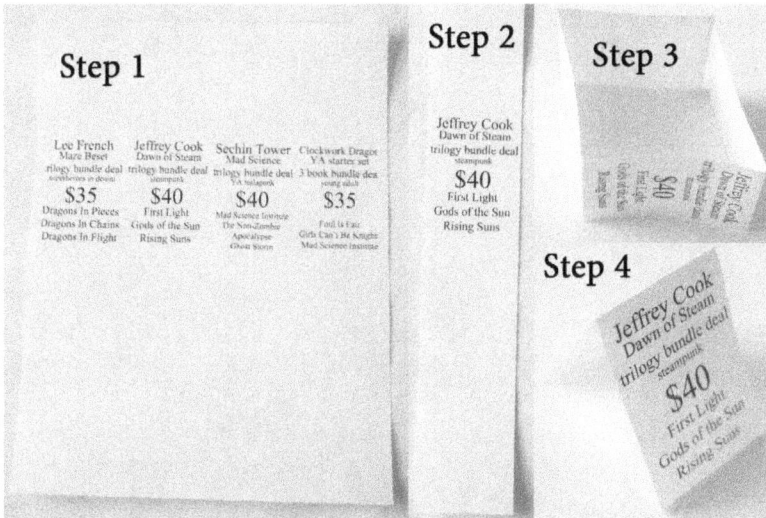

Information to include on these cards: The name of the series, the set deal price, and the names of the included books in series order. Because all the authors of Clockwork Dragon write in different genres, I like to include the subgenre information, such as "YA urban fantasy." I'm fond of using the same font as the book cover, but any clear, readable font works fine.

Place these cards where they can be clearly seen and associated with their set. I like to put them on top of the book 2 or 3 stack so they don't obscure the book 1 cover, or in front of the set if you're able to stage all the books in holders.

As a secondary option, we've also had some success with printed notes in cheap plastic picture stands. These look nice, but don't fit on the table in every situation, whereas we can always find space to use the pop-up placards.

Having a Presence

Lee: Your books and display aren't the only things at your table. Part of your job at a convention is selling an image of yourself as an author. Many people will buy a book from you because of you, not because of the book. This section discusses creating and maintaining a presence at your table.

Dress for Success

Jeff: "I love your hat."

We hear that all the time at conventions, because Lee and I each have really fancy, eye-catching hats that suit our genres and geekdoms. She made hers, mine was made by a local crafter who shares my love of steampunk. Regardless, they get the attention of people wandering by, make them stop, and tell customers something about us.

If you want a job as a lawyer, you show up for the job interview in your best suit. If you want to work at a record store, you show up in a band t-shirt to show you're passionate about music. Conventions are no different. When selling, you're conducting hundreds of mini-job interviews per weekend.

In every one of those, you want to convince the people at the conventions—in our case, fans of science fiction and fantasy—that you're one of them. You love what you're doing.

You enjoy the community. You have something to say in your books that's meaningful to them. The way to do this before saying a word is to dress like a geek, and further, in some way that draws attention and gives people some idea what they'll find in your books.

Lee: Some authors wear professional clothes, such as suits or nice dresses. Others wear t-shirts with their cover or related art. Still others wear geeky t-shirts proclaiming their favorite fandoms. Costuming is also popular. All these approaches are fine. The key is to appear presentable. Don't roll out of bed and go directly to your table without checking a mirror at least once.

It's generally helpful to have some facet of your professional persona that doesn't change much between conventions. For us, it's the hats. For others, it might be the shirts or kilts, or the colors you prefer. If you wear a costume, make it the same costume or collection of costumes at every con. Part of your goal is to be recognizable. If Jane Doe sees you first at Con X and later Con Y, you want her to make the connection as easily as possible, even if you change your hairstyle or start wearing contact lenses.

Jeff's Caveat: Conventions require standing and/or sitting for long periods of time in limited space. They also require setup, teardown, and maintenance of decorations and inventory during the show. You absolutely must be able to move around, use your hands freely, and comfortably spend hours in that space. Eye-catching costuming to show investment in what you're doing and your fandom is important, but make sure you can work in it.

Lee's Caveat: Some conventions are 4-5 days long. Whatever you choose to wear, make sure you can pack enough of it to wear fresh clothes as much as possible. Deodorant only goes so far. You will sweat during setup and teardown, you'll inevitably spill lunch or snacks on yourself, you may have to go outside during interesting weather, and so on. Plan for disaster.

Be There

Lee: Readers want to meet the writer and get their book signed in person. Publishing a book confers the mystical quality of "Author," and people want that to rub off on them. If you leave your table in the hands of someone else, no matter how good they are at selling your books, they aren't you. Some breaks are good, and even necessary. Spending zero time at your table isn't helpful.

Bottom line: if you don't care enough about your books to be there, no one else will either. Plan to spend at least half your con time working the table.

Jeff: In addition to simply being present at the table, be invested in your audience. Make sure someone at the table is paying attention and watching the people coming and going. If you don't look interested in what you're doing or like you want to talk to people, you'll get fewer customers approaching.

I mentioned it in an earlier section, but want to stress this here as well : even when it's slow, look awake, aware, and interested. This can be difficult when it's slow, especially. Remember, customers may well see you before you see them. Someone at the table should have their head up, keeping an eye on the room at all times.

Lee: The grumpy, introverted author may be a humorous cliché, but it doesn't attract people. If you happen to suffer from social anxieties or similar difficulties, find ways to practice meeting random people. Practice your pitches. Force yourself to deal with it, because selling books at conventions doesn't work if the only thing you can do is sit and hope no one tries to talk to you or wants to hear a book pitch.

Panels and Other Engagement

Jeff: This is one of those things that comes very easily for some people, and not as easily for others. Finding other ways to engage your audience can really help you. I try to do a couple of panels at most conventions I go to. This gives me a chance to speak to an audience, usually about topics I can speak on with at least moderate expertise—my usual panels include Steampunk 101, The History of Steam and Steampunk, and Writing YA fiction.

This helps me stand out to those people, and many of them will end up going through the merchant's room later. Yes, it's time away from the table, but used well, it can be a valuable investment of time.

If you're going to do this, though, you need 3 major things to make it work in terms of being a business investment.

1. You actually need to know your topic enough to speak on it for at least half an hour, and to be able to take questions.

2. You absolutely need someone at the table who can and will sell your books while you're gone.

3. You need to not do too many of these. The previous section still applies. If you're not at your table during the convention, the people who meet you in panels won't connect the person they heard speaking to that product. A few panels per convention are good, and can help your business model. Too many, and you're hurting your business venture.

Lee: Though I've been told the contrary, I'm not terribly good at this stuff. Being the focus of attention for a group of strangers makes me incredibly uncomfortable. However, I recognize the value of them, which is why I force myself to do them. After a reading, there's always at least one person who liked it and wants to get the book. That makes the time spent—which costs me nothing, because I have a partner to work the table in my absence—worthwhile.

Social Media

Lee: For conventions, the most useful social media are the ones the convention committee has an account for. Others may be personally useful for you, but this isn't about you. It's about the convention. They want you to attract people for the event, not to the bar afterward. If you want them to help you, you have to help them.

Before the con, don't spam them. Hit each relevant platform during the week prior to the con and use a picture of some sort, whether it's a book cover, your author picture, or a picture from a previous con. As soon as you're set up before the con, take a few pictures of your table, either in whole or partially. For best effect, get someone else to take it so you can be in the picture, especially if you wear a full or partial costume. Tweet one, tagging the con's handle and whatever hashtag they're using. Mention your table location. If you can, do the same with any other accounts they have an hour or two before the vendor's room opens, but using a different picture.

Where to go from here depends on your relationship with social media in general. It's a good idea to interact with the con's social media a few times over the course of the con, but only if doing so doesn't take away from being at the table or your general mental health. While you're off having lunch, try to remember to check their page and comment on something. As with all social media, don't sell, sell, sell. Be witty, funny, silly, or whatever else you usually are. Post pictures of cosplayers you encountered and cool displays.

For one-or-two-day events, this is sufficient. If it has three or more days, post something again on the morning of the last day. Remember to use pictures! The people running those accounts prefer picture posts over link or text posts, and are more likely to repost if you include pictures, especially amusing or interesting ones.

Selling Books

Lee: At this point, you're nearly ready to work your first convention. Now comes the delicate matter of selling your books to strangers. Holding up a book with a smile might work in some situations. More often, you need to engage a potential customer to turn them into an actual customer.

The Art of the Soft Sell

Lee: Earlier, you learned what the Soft Sell is and isn't, and now we'll discuss the how of Soft Selling. After that, we go much deeper into the why. It isn't only about avoiding the used car salesman smell. There's much more to it.

Jeff: Ultimately, Soft Selling is about convincing people to enter your sales space and look through your products. You're not yelling, you're not out in the aisles shoving books at them, and you're not telling them what you want them to buy. If people are in the vendor room, they're at least potentially interested in buying things there. You want them to drive most of the sales experience. Set out books in ways that catch attention and be helpful without getting in their face.

Your selling should largely be done at your table. If you're wandering around with a book in hand, you're probably not Soft Selling. If someone stops, and you immediately shove a book of your choice at them and go into your pitch, you're also not Soft Selling.

Things you should do:

1. Make sure someone at the table has their head up, looking interested in the people wandering by, and people at the table. You want to appear available and helpful. If you're going to check e-mail on your phone, that's fine, as long as someone at the table is in customer service mode. This can be really hard to do, especially during the long periods with no activity.

2. The first goal you want to keep in mind is to match customers with the book they want. Let them browse. See what catches their attention. Let them know you're there to answer questions, but don't press. If they want to engage you, answer their questions and show interest in them and what they're looking for.

3. Be courteous, and to the best of your ability, concentrate on one person at a time. If you need to engage someone else, apologize, and get back to the people you're helping in a timely fashion.

4. Don't press too hard to get anyone to buy something. A lot of people don't buy anything at all on their early passes through a vendor room, or until near the end of the convention. If you push too hard, you may not only lose

them when they weren't going to buy anything anyway, but also ensure they won't stop by your table later.

5. Catch attention with your display and make the space a comfortable place for customers to spend time in.

6. If anyone can talk about any book on the table, and everyone's first concern is matching customers to books, it promotes a less competitive atmosphere. If you're comfortable in the space, it will show.

Make the Environment Comfortable

Jeff: No, not for you. For the customer. Going in, you're probably not a bestselling author. Very few people will actively search you out for your books. You need to make people want to shop at your table. A big part of this is creating a comfort level there.

Let people browse through the books. Don't shove books under noses or shout about what a great book something is. Take note of what people look at. Nod or wave. Be friendly, and try not to be too aggressive.

Lee: A simple "Hello" with a smile is a great way to begin. Upon being verbally acknowledged, most people will make it clear if they intend to continue to browse or not. If you genuinely like their cosplay or some aspect of it, appreciating verbally it also works well. Caution: don't do that unless you actually like the thing you're pointing out. They'll see right through you if you're faking interest in them.

Jeff: If they do start talking to you, or looking through books for a while, start off with things like:

"I've read that one. That's a great book." (If it's not your own.)
"Can I help you find anything?"
"Please, feel free to look through the books."
"What types of books do you like to read?"

Let them guide the conversation when you can. Be casual, explain the books that they show the most interest in, and if they say something indicating their preferences, try to guide them to those books, even if they're not your own.

Lee: Do not ask "Are you a reader?". It's insulting and silly. If they stop to look at the books, they probably like to read. If they don't stop, you asking that question won't make them do so. They might ignore you or they might avoid you for the rest of the con. People shopping for friends or family will make their purpose clear and don't need you to ask.

A good follow-up to someone who says they're looking for "science fiction" or "fantasy," or an equally broad genre is to ask if they like one or more specific subgenre markers you happen to have on your table. For example, when someone tells me they like "fantasy," I often ask if they also like sarcasm. Those who say yes get pitched *The Greatest Sin*. Those with less enthusiasm for it hear about other books.

Some people are just browsing and don't want to talk to you. That's okay. Offer to answer any questions they might come up with, pay attention in case they do want anything, and return whatever gesture they offer if they choose to walk away. Many con-goers will make five or more passes through the Dealer's Room before they decide to buy anything.

When you do have a conversation, try to remember that customer's face whether they buy a book or not. Recognizing them later—in the bar, at a room party, even at a store or restaurant—may mean a future sale. If you can't remember everyone's names, don't fret. They probably won't remember yours, either. At least, not the first or second time you meet.

Geek Life

Jeff: A lot of people come to love science fiction and fantasy and the fandoms because compared to many social circles, it's an accepting one. Yes, it has its issues and jerks. Every population does. In general, though, a lot of people who may be ostracized elsewhere find a home among gamers and geeks.

Many of those people don't have a lot of confidence. More than a few have social anxieties or other issues that make dealing with people hard sometimes.

If you're selling to them, and especially if you want to keep selling to them, making them feel comfortable and relaxed in your workspace is essential. Yes, if you shove a book at them and start talking, you might make a sale of that book. As often as not, that's because they want you to go away. They'll avoid you and your booth in the future.

Talk to them about their fandoms, their games, their favorite books, and so on, and guide them towards the things they might like to read, while keeping things low-key. Whether you make a sale or not, you have made it much more likely they'll keep coming back.

In a few cases, that's because they now want to talk about their newest Drow ranger-assassin, but most often, it's because they had a good experience, and now they're invested in your books and your brand.

Lee: When in doubt, err on the side of not crowding them, either physically or socially. Nobody wants to be harassed by a used car salesman. You're left feeling slimy and pressured by that approach, and that goes double for introverts. Since you can't tell by looking whether someone has a social anxiety or not, treat everyone gently until they give you enough cues to run with.

Repeat Sales

Jeff: This is one of the core aspects of the business model we're working with, and so far, it's done well for us.

We're both fairly prolific authors, and we work with other authors as well. Repeat sales, people coming back for sequels, and people giving referrals to friends are all key to making conventions work for us.

Books aren't big margin items like cars or high-end artwork. One sale won't make a convention. You need to sell a good number of books to cover your costs for a convention. Then you need to do it again next event, and the next event. A high-pressure approach to make a single sale doesn't make sense with low-price items like this. The only way you're going to succeed is by bringing people back, whether to pick up the next books in series they've started or seeing what else is on the table.

Working primarily in one region, the Pacific Northwest, we see a lot of the same con-goers over and over. Some authors have the budget and business model that lets them travel a lot further and more often, but we can't do that, and I suspect most people just starting out are aiming to mostly do conventions in their area. With a limited and familiar customer base, if there are problems, word will get around. The same is true of making good connections. Do a good job in providing a comfortable space and making yourself memorable for the right reasons, and people will bring friends to your table. This is the very best kind of repeat customer.

Making Friends

Jeff: Almost every convention comes with a story. There's the one where we had a great sales convention, but were working out of way too little space. There's the convention we use as our low bar ("We're now officially better than X convention"—which shall remain nameless, but hang out with us and you'll know which one that is soon enough.)

Then there's the conventions that are memorable because of the people. In addition to selling your product, conventions are a great opportunity to network. You meet other vendors, work with other authors, meet the fans who get really into your work, and potentially discover people with contacts or skillsets that may come in handy for you later.

I'm also always looking for how I can create contacts via what I can do for other people within the limits of my time and contacts. I host networking events, and I've made a fair number of friends by inviting beginning authors to come have a table, make a few sales, and meet useful contacts. I make introductions between people. I invite sci-fi and fantasy authors to join Writerpunk Press, which may not make anyone (including me) any money, but it has helped several people gain confidence in their writing, get something published, and build contacts with editors, cover artists, etc. I go in and speak to classrooms if I can get there. We both give out our business cards freely and tell people they can contact us if there's anything we can answer.

To really take advantage of this aspect of conventions, you have to be genuine. People will see through it if you're not. But if you're sincerely willing to engage with people, there's a lot to be gained—especially goodwill—at conventions.

The one other thing I'll mention here is that conventions are one of the best chances you have to get a real sense of connection with your fans. Being an author is a lot of work, sometimes for very little reward. Treasure the experience and interaction. It really is a part of what makes being an author worthwhile.

Examples:

Most of the time when I go to Portland, which is a fairly long drive, one of my superfans shows up. She's started bringing friends by, and when she gets to my table, she's not at all quiet about it. This is *awesome* and gains all sorts of positive attention. Besides, the ego boost of being treated like a rock star, however briefly, is pretty cool.

One of our favorite regulars was someone we met at Gearcon. He bought a few books and came back the next day with helpful critique and mostly high praise. We complimented his steampunk craftwork and talked about subjects he was passionate about. We also praised his efforts at writing his own books and offered our help if he ever needed it. That person is now doing some crafting for us, helped us organize our own indie book fair on a college campus, and may even end up with his books on our table at some point in the future. He's an outstanding contact to have made, but that contact came very much out of a willingness to take the time to engage him about topics he was passionate about, showing an interest in what he had to say, and offering to help him—and demonstrating that we were willing to follow up when he called us on it.

And finally, the moment that made probably the second worst event of the year for me totally worth it. In writing *Foul is Fair*, I included some characters who, for various reasons, have really connected with readers who don't often see characters they can immediately identify with in most modern literature. Kerr, the brownie, is one of those characters. I'd done an event local to me that went fairly well, including talking to a group of teenagers who asked about some of the types of characters in the books. A couple of them did most of the talking, but they came up with a fair-sized group.

Cut to the next week, at the really not-as-fun event. There was a crowd, but very few sales. A teen, by themself, came up to the booth, speaking to me very, very quietly.

"I doubt you remember me, but I was at Maple Valley Days last week with my friends. They were asking about characters, and you answered them. I didn't buy the book then, but I did buy an ebook of Foul is Fair. When I saw you here, I just had to come up and say thank you for writing Kerr. There's finally someone in fiction like me. And I wanted to know if it would be ok to give you a hug?"

Given the chance, the people at a convention and the experiences of dealing with those people and trying to create a positive experience can end up being worth a lot more than a sale. To get there, though, you have to treat those people genuinely, with respect, and like they're worth a lot more to you than dollar signs.

Lee: I haven't been working events as long as Jeff has, so I only have one example. I worked a 4 day event by myself and had a young woman come by on Day 2. We chatted about a range of subjects, rambling across her favorite books and movies and all sorts of thing. She bought a copy of *Girls Can't Be Knights*. Day 4, she came back and exploded with joy all over me because she loved the book and wanted to make sure she shook my hand and got her book personalized, which she hadn't done when she bought it. While she gushed, she made sure to direct some of her gushing at the other person standing at my table and attracted attention from others nearby. Because of her, I made another sale I otherwise might not have.

Which One is Yours?

Jeff: So, if I'm selling other people's stuff on a regular basis, trying to match people with books, and Soft Selling, how do I ever sell my own books outside of random chance? Is it all really worth it?

The title of this section is also the answer. An amazing amount of the time, if you've created a good impression in people's minds, made them comfortable talking to you and being at your table, and convinced them that your primary goal is to help them find the book they want, they'll come around to this question.

All the time you spend selling other people's books or selling the table as a brand, you're actually selling your most important product: yourself. As an early-career indie author, these people don't know you. If you become, in their mind, the kind of author they want to read, people will take a chance on your books. Quite often, they'll do so even if they already have books by other authors in hand closer to what they wanted in terms of style and genre. What's more, they will be the ones who keep coming back.

One of the best examples of this came from one of my early shows. I spent quite a while talking to a customer, going through all the books. In the end, he held up two books. One of them was *Dawn of Steam: First Light,* the other was Victoria Bastedo's *Sunrise Meets the Star.*

Customer: I'm going to buy a book, but I only have enough money for one of these. This one (Victoria's) is more like what I typically read, and it sounds really good, but you're here.

Me: Then buy Vicky's book. I'll give you a card so you can contact her if you want it signed. She's a great lady.

He bought *Sunrise Meets the Star,* and he loved it. I know that, because I've seen that same customer several times since. He told me about it, and thanked me for the recommendation. Since then, he has also bought every book I've put out. The thing is, he actually did struggle when he started *Dawn of Steam: First Light*. It's not what he typically reads, and it's a really dense book—intentionally so, aimed at heavy readers. But that first sale built a level of trust, and by the time he got to reading it, he was invested in me as an author.

Lee: Often, when you match someone with a book, they'll set it in the crook of their arm and ask after your work. Having already found one thing they like can help you select one of your own books to offer them. If someone is interested in the romantic, grand, sweeping epic of *Dawn of Steam*, I'm not likely to suggest the action-packed superheroes of *Maze Beset*. Instead, I'll talk about *Al-Kabar*, which is written in a different style, but has more similar themes. Likewise, someone who's agog over *Foul Is Fair* will get pitched fellow Young Adult urban fantasy *Girls Can't Be Knights* over my more mature epic fantasy *The Greatest Sin* series.

Working the Room

Lee: Although working a convention room is similar to working retail, it's also quite different. The skillset and mindset of a retail manager can help you a great deal. It can also hinder you in some specific ways.

You Have No Competition in the Dealer's Room

Jeff: This is, strictly speaking, not entirely true. Buyers come to conventions with limited budgets. They're not going to buy something from everyone. The more accurate statement would be to say that it isn't worthwhile to treat the other vendors, even the booksellers, as if they were competition.

Firstly, because readers are readers. Very few of them buy just one book. Create a positive experience and make a good impression. Even if they don't buy this time, they might later. Being willing to refer someone to another vendor who has what they're looking for if you don't may even help you twice over: the other vendor may return the favor or help you out later, and you've built a degree of trust with that customer.

Secondly, because you're all in this together. And that's important. Making going to the dealer's room, in general, a positive experience for customers benefits everyone, and you're part of everyone.

Lee: Fights in the Dealer's Room, while uncommon, happen. They're horrible experiences, even for uninvolved parties. While it may be funny at the time, it sows the seeds of animosity. The dealers involved still have to see each other for the rest of that con and face the possibility of working adjoining booths at future cons. Everyone else sees the fight and is faced with the prospect of taking sides. No one wins in this case, especially if merchandise is damaged or destroyed in the argument.

It's also worth saying that when you're on good terms with other vendors, they may become your customers. When you're selling books, you can reasonably target anyone interested in your genre and sub-genre and know the other booksellers aren't offering the same thing. However, never push your books at other vendors. Vendors are there to make money, not spend it. They know all the routines and marketing tricks, so don't waste your time. If they want a book, they'll get a book, and it'll be because it's *your* book.

Information Trading

Jeff: Vendors talk to each other. If you've only ever gone to a convention as a guest, you haven't seen the long hours spent on setup and teardown. There's no one else to talk to. And, like pretty much every other group of people who get together at an event built around common interests, we talk about the things we have in common. Primarily, that's shows and customers.

If a vendor does very well at a convention, and you're friendly and conversational towards them, they will tell you about that convention. It might seem counter-intuitive at first, but consider it this way: the conventions are going to have the same number of dealers, regardless. Someone will be in those spots. So, the people who do a lot of conventions, in particular, want the people who are easiest to get along with, easiest to talk to and pass time with, and who will be honest with them about events and customers in those spots. More often than not, a good show is a good show for everyone, and a bad show is a bad show for everyone.

Lee: A friendly vendor might be willing to let you name-drop them on your application. You may learn who to contact to facilitate it and which words to use or offers to make. They'll answer questions, let you borrow tape, and lend a hand when you need it. Remember who helped you and return the favor when you can. They'll remember that you didn't take the help and run.

No One Else Understands

Jeff: Being overly competitive and hostile to your fellow vendors really puts you in a difficult spot. No one else understands the amount of work that goes into a convention, or dealing with customers. Your friends are at conventions to have fun. Odds are, they'd love for you to come hang out with them, do room parties, etc., and won't get it when you need some sleep, because you work early the next day. No one else wants to hear your rant about con-goers. Vendors sometimes do, and then will tell you their own.

Lee: When a con goes sour, these are the people who can relate. They've all got experience. Through conversations, a group of vendors can suss out the problems and report them en masse to the convention staff. Additionally, they're the people who've seen it all and can tell you if a particular happening is quite normal or completely bizarre.

Jeff: At the end of every convention, there's usually one last meeting for expressing what went well, and what didn't. Vendors presenting there as a bloc carry a lot more weight. If the experience hasn't been a good one, likely everyone, or almost everyone, has had the same difficulties. Being in a position to discuss those, think over what you're going to tell the con organizers, and have a bunch of people there agreeing with your points is helpful, in terms of the con organizers caring what you have to say. You and your booth might not mean a lot to the convention. The vendors as a whole, they care about.

You'll See Them Over and Over

Jeff: Do you like every one of your co-workers at your day job? Probably not. Do you understand that being able to work together in the same space is essential to anyone getting anything done? Probably.

Vendors at conventions are the same way. If you work a lot of conventions in your region, you'll become familiar with the same faces, and they'll get to know you. They will remember past experiences and react appropriately. You might not all sell the same things, but you're going to be in the same workplace over and over again.

Lee: When you're known among the vendors for being a jerk, no matter how friendly and cheerful you are to customers, you get treated like a jerk. Some vendors will purposely subvert you in small ways, such as mentioning they had a bad experience with that vendor in the corner over there. They may also do it accidentally, through a conversation they're unaware is being overheard. Others might only steer their friends away, but those friends will talk, and pretty soon, you're sitting by yourself with only a few token sales.

Conversely, if you're known for something positive, you'll be treated according to that. You may not get big sales because of it, but no one says bad things about the friendly vendor. Don't go out of your way to be super-nice or super-friendly, or super-anything, unless that's your thing. Do offer a hand to anyone who appears to need it, regardless of who they are, and be polite.

Above all, be genuine. If you're helping someone because you want a favor, people pick up on that. Get into the mindset of helping people just because you want to help people, and you'll do well. Of course, it's okay to completely fangirl/boy squee all over your heroes, just try to wait until they're not pulling a wagon full of stuff through a too small door or standing in line for the bathroom.

Important point: Never knowingly interrupt another vendor pitching to a customer. It's incredibly rude to try to "steal" a customer, even if you can't stand the vendor or know their product is low quality. That vendor will—guaranteed—return the favor, probably three-fold.

Volunteers and Con-Staff

Jeff: These people talk, both good and bad. You want to be friendly with the volunteers and anyone associated with the convention, period. Even if you're not planning on coming back, the same people are often associated with multiple conventions, or know people who are. Being friendly, helpful, and respectful will pay off in the long run. Resolve problems (and they will happen) calmly, and treat them like people. Particularly because, if a problem does arise, the person you have access to is probably not at fault, but is still expected to find a solution—so blaming them is pointless, and you want them to want to help you.

Lee: It's really important to emphasize that whatever goes wrong usually isn't the volunteers' fault. They're exactly like the customer service rep you talk to on the phone who has to explain how their company's policy on returns doesn't cover your accidental mashed potato incident. These people don't make the rules, and they can't break them for you, no matter how much they might like you. What they can do is alert the convention staff to a problem. Which they won't bother doing if you're a jerk about it.

Jeff: Volunteers in particular are sacrificing their fun time at the convention to help out. Be nice to them. If you're at a convention that collects swag for the volunteers, try and donate something, even if it hasn't been a great convention. Odds are, if it hasn't been a great convention, they've gotten plenty of backlash already, once again, for things that aren't their fault. So there's your chance to bite the bullet a little, and be the nice guy. You'd be kind of surprised how that can pay off. No guarantee that it will, but again, the people who are doing work behind the scenes do talk to each other.

Working With Helpers

Jeff: Many vendors have the occasional bit of help from friends or family. But how best to use the help when you have it?

You know your situation best, but here are my thoughts:

1. Make sure friends and family have a chance to enjoy the convention. Unless they're part of the business, don't overuse them. It's your responsibility to sell your books. If they're paying for a badge, encourage them to have some

fun at the con where possible.

2. You don't really want people behind the table who don't know the books unless you really need the help. Anyone who is going to be working the table for long periods should be someone who has taken the time to familiarize themselves with what's on the table. If a family member really wants to do that, great. You're not helping yourself much otherwise, though.

3. Setup and teardown are often great times to have some help. Lee would probably disagree, because she has a system, and is super efficient. For me in particular, and probably a lot of other authors, though, those are good times to have a spare set of hands or three.

   Lee: In fairness, until I had a system, I did appreciate the help. There are plenty of things people can still do to help me, and I let them. Because I do have a system, though, and Jeff is the only person I work with frequently enough to learn parts of it, it's generally quicker and easier for me to do it myself. When you work with a partner all the time, you'll find ways to get into a groove for setup and teardown that works for you.

4. "Booth Babes": some people object to the term and to the use of women in skimpy or flashy cosplay to draw attention to booths. For the purposes of this guide, we're

not specifically endorsing the idea: we're saying the term exists in con circles, and while it started out meaning a specific thing, many now use it to mean anyone who, through their appearance, costuming, accessories, etc. is used to draw attention to a booth. If you have friends who will dress as your characters, or even just have some amazing cosplay that people like to take pictures of, you can always see if they'll spend some time hanging out at your table.

Lee: The important thing to remember with this sort of attraction is to avoid the stereotypical booth babe: an attractive woman who does little more than show off her sparkling teeth and lots of skin. Sex may sell, but this sort of thing leaves a bitter taste with many potential customers, especially female ones. If you have someone eager to cosplay for you, make sure it's tasteful and appropriate for your image, comfort level, audience, and books.

5. Here's the one I never, ever would have guessed, but might be the most useful people we've had assisting us at conventions. The random people who will come hang out at the table on the customer side. It's good to have a friend chatting and providing an extra voice during those long, boring stretches. Even better is someone making you look busier than you are. Nothing draws attention like attention. These people are doubly helpful if they're aware enough to step aside when customers show up.

Jeff: Inevitably, there will be blockades. People run into friends in the vendor room and stop to chat. All too often, this happens right in front of your booth and can last hours. When the vendor asks them to move, you're branded as "rude," and they'll let people know it. Random passer-by, who happens to secretly be your friend, can politely ask them to move or not block the aisle without it coming back on a particular booth.

6. Have a plan. If you are going to get help moving things, setting up, tearing down, or having someone at the table, have a plan. Because there are things I'm not really capable of doing on a consistent basis, when I do have to work a convention mostly on my own, I come in knowing at least the basics of what goes where and what needs to happen. Similarly, I know the con hours, and when I'm familiar with a show, I try and remember when it was busiest, or what particular challenges came up.

When Things Go Wrong

Jeff: To this point, there's been a lot about things to do and how to approach things. Following the suggestions we've detailed—and learning as we've made mistakes and done more conventions—has helped us avoid a lot of problems. The truth is, though, something will go wrong at almost every convention. Sometimes it's the convention's fault, sometimes it's your fault, and sometimes, fate just conspires to make things interesting. Trying to cover every possible way things could go wrong is pointless—there will always be new problems. Instead, I'll start out with some broad-strokes steps that apply to almost every situation, and some things that will be useful regardless. After that, I'll try to list a few of the more common situations we've run into and potential ways to deal with them.

Above all, keep your cool and be polite.

Jeff: I really cannot stress this enough. If things go wrong, regardless of how, if you need to step outside and cuss, complain, vent, pace, whatever, do that. Do not yell or make a scene in the vendor room, and calm down before figuring out how to deal with a situation.

Though they're often the most convenient to blame, vendor room liaisons didn't make all the rules. The volunteers have no say in policy. Aside from that, it absolutely will hurt you in the long run if you lose your temper at them. The same people are often involved with multiple conventions in your area. Almost every convention keeps a "Do Not Invite" list. If you're rude to staff, yell at volunteers, make situations worse, or cause major disruptions, even if you were wronged in some fashion, the convention organizers will hear about it. Once they do, you may not be welcome back at that convention, or you may find your applications rejected by other conventions.

On the other hand, if you approach staff politely, address the situation, and look for alternatives, they may be able to help you. Even if they can't help out in a particular situation, you may earn some goodwill that will benefit you in the future.

Lee: If you aren't stellar at the people thing, and you need to deal with this stuff, remember that the con staff are also fellow human beings. They're probably geeky in some fashion, or they wouldn't have gotten involved in a convention. No matter what else is true, you have something in common with them and a common ground to work from.

The important thing is to remain professional. When you're professional, they take the cue and react professionally. Your problem gets solved—or at least addressed—and you don't become a problem yourself.

If someone on con staff acts unprofessionally toward you, disengage and seek another member of the con staff. When it's an attendee behaving like a jerk, making inappropriate advances, or doing anything else that makes you feel threatened, you still need to keep your cool. Stay safe, get their badge name, and alert con staff as soon as you can.

Allow yourself more time than you think you'll need.

Jeff: When you find out the dealer room's setup hours, try to get there as early as possible. We go into every convention assuming that we will need to adjust to something. It may be the amount of space, something missing from your convention gear, or slow lines to get your dealer badges. Give yourself enough time to make adjustments. If everything is fine, then you can talk to people, settle in, and catch your breath before things open. Book tables, once you get used to them, usually don't take long to set up, but the vendor room setup hours are still part of your work schedule. Use them.

Lee usually arrives before I do now—she handles the majority of setup and prefers to do so. Even without that, I try to show up early enough to meet the dealer room liaison and any volunteers working the room, get a feel for the space, check in with Lee, meet our neighbors, and see what's around us. I also really prefer to settle in for at least fifteen minutes to mentally "shift gears" from setup to room opening.

Among other things, use this time for a final test of your technology. If you're using a Square reader to accept credit cards, make sure it's working. Get the wifi password and determine if the connection is good enough. You'll be glad you did the tests before you end up telling a customer that, yes, you can take card, only to have to fiddle with your phone for ten minutes.

Lee: I plan for setup to take 4 hours from whenever I walk into the con to the table being ready for sales. The actual setup part can take anywhere from half an hour to 2 hours, depending upon the size of the space we have to fill. Other matters to consider: parking, the distance between your car and your table, finding the nearest and next nearest bathrooms, finding any rooms you have panels or workshops in, stowing all your cases and boxes out of sight, and arranging your space behind the table so you have everything you'll need frequently close at hand.

If you don't have wifi in the dealer room, and you use a credit card reader, don't panic. Square can still run cards in offline mode. When you're forced to do so, get every credit customer's name, phone number, zip code, card number, and purchase amount on a piece of paper. You'll need all this information if the card is rejected later.

Treat staff as allies whenever possible.

Jeff: Conventions, in general, want vendors to be happy. Vendors provide a significant portion of their guaranteed income and draw. Most are aware that the vendors talk to each other, and word will get around about major problems. If they don't have vendors, they lose interest from con-goers. They also lose money. This doesn't mean they're going to bend over backward to make any single vendor happy, but if there's a problem, most con staffers would like to see it solved.

Conventions have dealer room liaisons for a reason. At the most cynical level, that reason is insulating other people from being yelled at. It's also because conventions are aware that in limited space and with a lot of moving parts—figuratively and literally—things go wrong. It's best to have someone there to help deal with the problems.

For a lot of issues you're likely to run into, most dealer room liaisons have probably seen something similar before and have experience dealing with the issue. Even if they can't do anything about a particular problem, it doesn't hurt you and may benefit both you and the dealers in general to at least make the convention staff aware of potential problems or issues they may be able to avoid in future years.

Do this from the beginning. Part of my setup time goes to talking to staff, especially the room liaison, if they have time, and ask if there's anything we should be aware of.

Lee: It's worthwhile to find a few minutes here and there to chat with con staff and volunteers, provided they have time. Never interrupt them from their job to geek out over the latest movie, but if you see them at a good time to do so, don't be afraid to ask about the button, shirt, scarf, badge ribbon, or whatever else they're wearing that interests you. As with customers, though, keep it genuine. Build a rapport whenever you can.

Communicate.

Jeff: Whenever space is at all likely to be a concern, I make sure to include on applications that I'm handicapped, I cannot stand throughout a convention and need reasonable space to get around. If there is something you absolutely need to have accommodated, let them know. Likewise, if you see potential concerns or possible ways to improve, politely tell a member of the staff.

Talk to your neighbors when they're not obviously busy setting up. Take into account any concerns they might have, and particularly take note if they're familiar with that convention.

Just as importantly, use the quiet stretches to communicate with people working your table. Make sure you know what's going on, any concerns they have, if they need to take a break, and so on. Part of working a table together is being on the same team.

If the problem is someone else's, help out if you can.

Jeff: Lee is super efficient at setup at this point. We're often one of the first ones ready to go, especially if she's mostly doing setup alone. More than once, she's ended up loaning out tape, lending a quick hand elsewhere, etc. This earns goodwill and makes for friendlier neighbors in a lot of cases.

Similarly, at a recent Worldcon, someone had a few high-value items stolen. Virtually everyone in the vendor area spread the word and helped keep an eye out for the missing items. Thieves are a problem for everyone.

When people are running booths alone, when possible, one of us will step in to watch other people's booths so they can stretch, grab food, or use the facilities. We can't take sales for them, but we can make sure merchandise doesn't walk away and let customers know that the vendor will be back soon.

If the problem is another vendor, make sure you're covered.

Jeff: Sometimes conflicts erupt between vendors. This is a terrible situation for everyone involved, and makes everyone look bad. This can come up for any number of reasons. Whatever it is, if it's a minor issue, bring it up politely. We've had issues with people's displays ending up encroaching into our booth. A few polite words dealt with the situation.

If someone doesn't stop problematic behavior, if the issue is a bigger thing, or if you have reason to think someone might take offense, quietly let staff know what's going on. Either let them deal with it, or, if you still end up needing to address it, at least staff knows you reported the problem and asked for assistance or advice first.

The convention will ultimately do what is best for the convention, or what is perceived as best. If two vendors have a conflict and it disrupts business or the running of the convention, both parties may be asked to leave or put under extra restrictions. Keep yourself ahead of this by making sure the convention staff knows you're attempting to be reasonable and helpful.

Lee: For most minor issues, other vendors are usually reasonable, and you can hash things out yourselves. I've been in a situation where one of my table-mates had a severe allergy attack triggered by the actions of the next vendor over. A quick chat with the other vendor solved the problem—in fact, she was mortified. If you discover a similar situation and the vendor isn't willing to be reasonable, figure out what would solve the problem and take the issue to the dealer liaison. Health issues trump annoyances in all cases.

Apologies cost nothing, and can earn a lot in return.

Jeff: If you or someone associated with your booth causes a problem, or is perceived to have caused a problem, don't be shy about taking the initiative and apologizing. Even when it's not your specific fault, everyone at the table represents you, and vice versa. If one person causes enough issues, everyone may be asked to leave or blacklisted. An apology will go a long way toward either soothing hurt feelings, or, at a minimum, clearing your personal name.

There's a principle I learned while working a decade in customer service. It applies to a number of the above points, but I'm putting it here, because apologizing to people is a first step in this process.

The companies whose customers never have problems with either products or services rarely have the highest customer satisfaction ratings. For those companies, most customers rate them as "satisfactory," or "good."

The places that earn top marks are the ones where problems come up and someone representing the company took the time and effort to provide a solution. Those are, most often, the places that earn the ratings of "great!" or "exceeds expectations."

I've worked with quite a few different people already, beyond just Lee. We've had the situation arise where someone working our table caused a problem for some of the convention staff. After I was made aware of it, I went and apologized directly to the staff members involved. I had no control over the situation, and it wasn't anything that I did directly, but I still took responsibility for it as a representative of Clockwork Dragon and our table.

Afterward, I got excellent feedback from staff, and it gave me a chance to make a good impression on people who otherwise wouldn't have recognized me at all.

Additionally, in illustrating points above, we actually only learned about this situation because we'd taken the time to get to know the dealer room liason, so when the staff considered listing us as not welcome back next year, she stepped up on our behalf and made us aware of what happened. We know for a fact that a lot of those people are involved in other roles with other conventions in the area as well.

Lee: Although it sounds harsh, your name and reputation, and that of any group you're working with, are more important than someone else's name and reputation. When one person causes a problem for a group, the group needs to salvage the *group's* name and reputation. It may become necessary to distance yourself and the group from the problem person, even if it's only from the con's perspective. Take care doing this, as the problem person may be a valuable part of your group for other reasons.

Build a consensus

Jeff: This goes back to all vendors being each other's best allies. If there's a problem that has a negative impact on everyone, make sure everyone takes that to staff, or, at worst, the "how can we improve?" meeting after the convention. A lot of voices together speak louder than one or two.

Common Problems

Jeff: If you work enough conventions, the following situations are likely to come up eventually:

Space limitations.

Jeff: Sometimes conventions try to cram as many vendors—their one guaranteed source of income—into a room as possible. This can lead to feeling very cramped, not having enough room to sit comfortably, roadblocks and traffic jams, customers not being able to easily access some tables, or difficulty moving around.

In an unusual case of this, we ended up with half a table due to a misunderstanding and had to share space with an unfamiliar neighbor who'd had the same misunderstanding. We and our tablemate took the problem to the dealer room liaison. There was, unfortunately, nothing they could do. Despite that, we handled it politely and then did our best with the space we had. It turned out to be an excellent show for sales, and we were specifically sought out to receive an invitation for the next year because we'd handled the situation without causing a fuss.

Once dealers are booked, there's not usually much that can be done at the convention. Your best bet in this case is to consensus build and take the problem to the convention jointly, asking for either more space or fewer vendor spaces.

In a lot of conventions, this is a cyclical problem. They'll start out trying to make vendors comfortable. Something will shift and they'll invite a few more each year until it's way too crowded. When there are enough complaints, they ease back and it starts all over again.

Lee: In another example of unexpected space issues, my first Norwescon was spent working a group table, and we'd been set in front of the folded-up conference room dividers. This meant that, while everyone else had at least a 6x6 space to work with, we had 6x2. There was no space for displays behind us and barely enough space for the backstock of books, let alone people. Someone as tall as Jeff wouldn't have fit behind our table. There was nothing the dealer room liaison could do, as the vendor room was full and had zero no-shows. We had to make do with what we got.

Never expect to have any more space than the application says. When you get a 10x10 booth, that doesn't mean you should expect a corner. When you get a 6 foot table, the only way to know how much space you'll actually have behind it is to show up. Even when you ask in advance, you may not get the final answer, as things can change up to the day of the con. Plan for your best case and expect your worst case.

Interpersonal Conflict

Jeff: Some people just aren't going to get along. Others will rub you the wrong way. I've mentioned a couple of people I've worked with in the past where our approaches just didn't mesh well.

We had a problem in one of my earliest networked events where one of the authors consistently interrupted other conversations to very firmly push their own books. We had another where I, unfortunately, failed in terms of table assignments when everyone had to share a table with one other author, and I placed one very loud, firm person beside someone with social anxiety.

In the latter case, other people tried to help the quieter person, pointing a few customers their way and making introductions, as well as trying to provide chances to get away from some of the chaos.

In the former case, there were efforts made to talk to the person, which didn't change much. In the end, everyone involved made sure not to invite them to future sales events. That particular author may have done fairly well that day, but in the long run, cost themselves opportunities to sell books and have people recommending them.

At the time, I worried that asking them to leave would cause a scene and other issues. That may have been true. On the other hand, I know at least one friend of mine with some social anxiety issues felt pressured into a sale by that author. They bought a book in the hopes that would make the person go away. The book was donated to a library, otherwise unread, and my friend now prefers not to attend these types of events. That, as much as anything, means I'm less likely to be as charitable with these kinds of issues at future events.

Be very aware of any issues or irritations surrounding people you share a table with repeatedly. Try and settle things outside of the conventions, and, if necessary, seek out different table-mates. Whether family, close friends, or business partners, any people who spend a lot of time in close proximity will inevitably end up with some kind of conflicts. This isn't to say any partnership is doomed, only that something you disagree on will inevitably arise. Don't cause unnecessary drama when those do come up, and try to be mature about dealing with them. Make sure you're on the same page with people you intend to work with, and if your approaches don't fit, or you're pushing their work and the effort doesn't go both ways, you're probably best riding out that convention. Afterward, either try to clear up any miscommunications or find other people to work with.

Lee: The absolute most important point here, specifically with regards to table-mates, is to not hash anything out in the dealer room during show floor hours. Take it outside, as I tell my kids. Agree to disagree during the show, get it done, then settle up later. Try your best to be the better person at the time, even when you'd rather be a jerk. Remember, even if you have a falling out with a table-mate, you still may see them at the next con, whether they're at your table or a different one. Because conventions are scheduled up to a year in advance, you may have trouble avoiding them for a while.

That said, if you've gotten yourself into a partnership and the two of you wind up with an irreconcilable argument, get out of that partnership. This is about your livelihood and your mental health. You may have to forgo working an event or find someone else or another table space on short notice. That stress is better than long-term interpersonal stress.

Stolen merchandise

Jeff: Thankfully, this happens less often than you'd think. Because it's the biggest worry of most vendors and conventions, there tend to be a lot of precautions taken. Many conventions lock up the vendor hall once people leave for the day. Vendors tend watch out for each other where this is concerned.

However, something going missing eventually is inevitable. Books are, unfortunately, easily portable items, and it's not at all unusual to see people wandering around conventions with books in their bags.

Take inventory and be aware of what's on the table.

Keep an eye on people passing by. Report stolen items. During room hours, your best weapon is paying attention to what's going on around you.

Lee: Thefts occasionally happen between vendors. If you return in the morning and find something missing from the night before, first double-check your inventory to make sure you aren't remembering wrong. Then report it immediately to the dealer liaison. Don't try to figure it out or handle it on your own without at least consulting them. While you may be capable of handling the issue just fine, the con staff needs to know about it. If you say nothing and just quietly threaten the other vendor, you may never have a problem with them again, but that does nothing to help the other vendors at the next con. Be the hero for the vendor room and word will get around.

Damaged Goods

Jeff: Sooner or later, every author who goes to conventions has to deal with this one. Sometimes it's minor, but when your income is small, any loss hurts. Other times, it's a lot worse.

This is mostly mitigated by planning and careful packing. Tightly packed boxes, waterproof containers, and use of packing material like foam and cardboard are your friends.

My first year at Orycon was a killer for me. I was lucky to find some people willing to pick up readable material 'at cost', at least replacing the books, but that first bus trip meant I went into the convention with only half of the books I was hoping to put on the shelves. When I "sold out" of my stock at the convention, I had some trouble explaining to others why it wasn't much of a reason to celebrate.

I've certainly heard far worse stories as well.

When it does happen, hope you're close enough to home to replace books. Sell damaged goods cheap if you can to try to replace the stock, as long as they're still readable. Try to figure out how to pack better next time. When it can be avoided, stick with transportation methods where you have some control over where your things are stored and how they're kept. You also have my sympathy.

Lee: Even if you prepare and do everything you can to avoid damage, you can still always find a few books with manufacturing defects while on the road. Accidents happen between the car and the loading dock. You might be unlucky enough to spill your water bottle that you thought was closed all over a stack of books.

Salvage what you can and use books with minor damage as display copies. If they're still readable but not saleable, or you're not comfortable selling them even at cost, consider writing a note on the front page about how the damage happened—a short, amusing sentence or two is best—and setting them on the freebie table. Make sure you sign any such copies. Some people will cherish the coffee-stained or water-damaged book as a one-of-a-kind memento of a convention.

If you *are* comfortable selling damaged books—or

proofs, printing error copies, or old editions—at or slightly above cost, set them together in a container with a sign clearly indicating such. Do not mix them in with the other books. A basket, shoebox, or similar container will work fine, so long as all the cheap books are together. Generally, offer such books for the higher of $5 or the cost rounded up to the nearest dollar.

The Aftermath

Jeff: Just as you spend a lot of time stocking up, gearing up, and getting ready for a convention, what you do afterward is important. The following sections are mostly about following through and getting as much value out of a convention as possible.

Financial Expectations

Jeff: When looking back at a convention, stay realistic. Conventions are tremendously helpful for getting books out there, building your fan-base, interacting with fans and seeing the reactions, and sometimes even making money. But you have to keep all the expenses in mind. You'll need:

1. to replace the books you sold.

2. food and drink at a convention. You may or may not have paid for a hotel. You also have travel costs.

3. to pay off the things you used to improve your presence at the convention. All those bookmarks, banners, and so on do cost something.

With those in mind, and the fickle nature of

conventions, you're not likely to start turning a profit right away. This is especially true if you only have 1 or 2 books out. That doesn't mean you shouldn't do it. Building your brand and making fans you wouldn't reach online or in your local community is valuable, and you'll sell more books to these same people later. Just go in knowing that's what you're doing.

Lee: The primary goal of a convention or other in-person book selling event is actually to break even. You want your sales to cover the costs, plus some amount to go towards the costs of your durable displays. Making a genuine profit of more than a few dollars, especially early in your career, is a reason to cheer.

It cannot be emphasized enough that conventions are not a wildly profitable enterprise for authors. Some vendors do very well and run their entire business through conventions. They aren't authors. You're not selling high-margin costuming gear or jewelry. Books are relatively low-margin goods, and your profits will be small. Your true purpose is to be seen, to connect with readers, to network, and to build your fan base.

Even big name authors don't make fabulous wads of cash on conventions. They have big budget displays, big piles of books, and big expenses. Unless a big name scores a Guest of Honor for a convention, he's got to get a badge, pay for a booth, and pay for travel. Even if he does, he's still got to get all his books and display out there, take time away from writing, manage the table, pay someone to manage things for him so he can scribble his name hurriedly on anything shoved under his nose, and probably host a room party.

In short, no author does this for the money.

Evaluating a Con for the Future

Jeff: The sad fact is, not every convention is a good fit for every author. There's also the level of trying to do too much. When a convention is over, take some time to reflect and discuss with the other authors at your table. Talk to other vendors when you get the chance. Was there something you could have done better? Did no one do well? Did books just not do well?

Conventions are expensive, and if you do several in the same area, there are repeat attendees. Figuring out what kind of audience is showing up—and if you can really call it worthwhile—is important. This is especially true early on when you're treating conventions as an investment more than a money-maker.

Lee: If you go to multiple conventions in the same area and see all the same faces in the customer base, that's a reason to scale back. It's fun to be there, and it's fun to connect with the same people all the time, but they aren't going to buy books from you every other month. A good rule of thumb is to avoid doing more than one per quarter in the same city, unless the foci of the cons are wildly different.

I'd work a comic con, a sci-fi con, and a fantasy con for three weekends in a row in the same city, but I wouldn't do two sci-fi cons in the same city within a few months of each other without a good reason. Sub-genre niche conventions, such as steampunk ones, are usually safe at any time if you have books in that sub-genre or a related one.

Jeff: Some conventions do have value beyond the immediately obvious. Locally, for example, I will always go to Norwescon. A lot of my friends attend Norwescon, including some I only see once or twice a year. I make the usual number of sales to unknown customers, but also have friendly contacts coming by the table and buying books, as well as hanging out and talking. If another event was scheduled right around that time, I'd give it a try.

Orycon is another example of a con with value beyond sales numbers. We both belong to the Northwest Independent Writers Association (NIWA). Orycon is their primary convention of the year, where they release their latest anthology and have a big room party. This is a chance to network with people we don't see very often and to work with and help people who are generally inclined to help us out as well.

Lee: Don't consider a particular event a failure just because you didn't make a profit, especially when you first start. Like cover art, editors, and marketing, this is an expense you'll have to bide your time to get back. Did you make good contacts? Did you create a fan or two? Did you learn something you can apply to your next appearance? Did you get invited to submit to a worthwhile anthology? Do you think the audience is there, but your display didn't pull them in? If you did sell a lot of books, was the reason you didn't make your expenses related to spending more than necessary on food or travel, or including promotional costs that could instead be spread out over several events?

Deciding whether to return the next year should be based on the overall picture of how the event went for you, not just the money. That one con where you made a contact for an incredible artist who will do your next cover on the cheap might be worth sticking with, especially if you think you can do better next time.

Jeff: Here's the additional value in working a convention with someone else. After any convention, Lee and I don't usually just independently talk about the convention on a yea or nay basis: we talk about the convention in general. We each see if the other picked up any new ideas or noticed anything we need to change, and confirm our impressions.

We're usually on the same page, but a second perspective can add a lot. Sometimes we simply agree that a convention is—or isn't—worth doing again. But most of the time, we at least gain some lesson in how to do things better, things to try, or things we should follow up on.

Take Care of Yourself

Lee: There's a phenomenon associated with conventions called "con crud." Between sharing a space with hundreds or thousands of strangers, working hard, not getting enough sleep, and either driving every day or staying in a strange place, many, many people get sick with a generic cold or flu after a convention. Do whatever you can to keep yourself healthy without putting off customers. Eat well and drink plenty of liquids.

Even if working a convention seems energizing at the time, Monday morning will probably feel like someone dropped a load of bricks on your head. Plan recovery time for the day after any convention, no matter how long it lasts. If you need to travel after the con, fold in enough time for a good night of sleep, either before you leave or after you reach your destination.

Managing Inventory

Lee: When you're first starting, inventory is a big deal, financially speaking. Every book has to be paid for out-of-pocket, and you need to pay that weeks in advance of the next convention. You'll have to make decisions about how many books you need with no idea how many you'll sell at any given event.

Uncertainty can't stop you from having books on hand.

Once you have a plan for how many books you'll need for your events, you need to store them someplace, in some kind of containers. Keep your books protected from sun, dampness, unwary shins and toes, toddlers, pets, food, and other disasters. When you have three or fewer titles, this probably means a box in the corner of a bedroom. When you have as many books as Jeff and I do, and are working events all the time, this can become a major issue requiring significant thought and effort.

Even more important than finding a safe place to keep your books and display materials is keeping track of your inventory. You need to know you're down to three copies of your best selling book *before* you pack for your next event. With the time it takes to get new copies from Print On Demand services, you need to know *three weeks* beforehand. If you're not good at keeping that sort of information in your head, or have several different titles, use a spreadsheet or other software. Square can manage this for you.

Ideally, your post-show routine should go something like this:

1. Remove the profits from your cash and restore your change to the right level.

2. Make sure your cash and credit card payments equal the amount of books you sold. Note discrepancies so you can claim losses on your taxes.

3. Keep track of any sales taxes you collected.

4. If you work with one or more partners, make sure everyone gets paid the proper amount.

5. Update your book inventory and re-order as needed.

6. Check your swag inventory and re-order anything you're getting low on.

7. Repair any damaged display items.

8. Repack everything for the next show and stow it in a safe place.

At some shows, you may need to pay collected sales tax at the end of the con. You'll be alerted to this by con staff prior to the event. Otherwise, keep records and set that money aside.

Conclusion

Jeff: I've had the opportunity in the past few years to talk to a lot of authors, particularly new and indie authors. Many see conventions and public events as scary. Others wonder about their value and if the investment is worth it.

Ultimately, my answer is that they can be, if you approach them in a professional manner and treat them as an investment in yourself and your books.

Conventions offer an unparalleled opportunity to interact with fans, both new and established. They also provide an opportunity to market yourself and your work more directly than through most other channels. There are ways to use different talents—whether you're a skilled organizer, planner, speaker, people-person, or something else. Conventions are also a tremendous opportunity to network. There are plenty of other authors and artists—and chances for inspiration and interaction with people who share your interests.

With patience, persistence, a quality body of work, a plan, and the right people, conventions can be a great way to build a fanbase, while hopefully at least breaking even and maybe even making a little money. As Lee noted, are you likely to get rich off of conventions? No, not likely. They're one tool in an author's arsenal for working towards the day you can make a sustainable living off your books.

We hope we've provided you some useful information

towards that goal. We've tried to not only explain what we do, but why we think it works. Whatever else you do, when approaching the idea of doing conventions, do your best to familiarize yourself with the convention. Know how many people are attending, what sort of accommodations are available, and if you'll have help. Check out the website. See what guests they've invited to get an idea of the audience the con is hoping will attend. Talk to other authors who've attended the convention before. Similarly, talk to friends who've gone to the convention as guests. Consider signing up for a panel or two, especially if you have at least one literary topic you feel you can speak on as an expert.

Then, after all the professionalism, planning, and the rest, try to have some fun. Talk to people about something you've put a lot of work into. Support other authors and artists —and hopefully get some support from them in return. If you write in a genre suitable for the convention, you'll be surrounded by things you enjoy. If you haven't been to many conventions, let others cover the table and go to a couple of panels, wander the dealer hall, or enjoy convention programming. Then take your turn covering the table so the people with you can do the same. If you're taking it seriously, you're working. On the other hand, you're also—in theory— getting paid to attend a convention.

Maybe I'm looking forward to the point when I'm doing 10-15 event weekends a year instead of 30, on top of writing and marketing online, because I can make a sustainable living without the constant road-warrioring. But I still want to work those once-a-month events and get the live feedback and connections.

I think we've found a way to make conventions work for us, and wherever our writing careers go, they'll always be a part of the plan. And for all that they're part of the business, there's a lot of fun to be had at them. Those times when you get to meet and interact with an excited fan, or connect with someone and make a new one, and chances to network and turn a mostly solitary career a little more social, make them worthwhile on top of the business sense.

I suspect, should you take the leap in your career to add a few live events to your schedule, that if you do actually do the legwork and go in with a plan, you'll ultimately find the convention experience more rewarding, easier, and even, for all the work involved, more fun too.

Lee: When you do start working conventions, if you see us, stop and introduce yourself. We're always happy to chat, answer questions, and share intel. Our goal is to make convention dealer rooms more pleasant and profitable for everyone, not just ourselves.

Checklists

Gear

Essential

Display case
Cart, wagon, or dolly
Book holders
Tablecloth
Safety pins
Pens
Credit card reader
Change for cash customers
Price stickers or price sheet with display method
Water bottle
Clipboard
Newsletter signup sheet
Business cards

Helpful

Duct tape
Scotch tape
Zip ties
Rubber bands
Cloth tape
Scissors
Cash box
Bookmarks
Other swag
Blank paper
Bedsheet or flat tablecloth

Contingent

Table
Swag holder
Shopping bags
Gallon freezer bags
Standing mat
book rack
Riser(s)
Backdrop

Post-Con Routine

1. Remove the profits from your cash to restore your change to the right level.

2. Make sure your cash and credit card payments equal the amount of books you sold. Note discrepancies so you can claim losses on your taxes.

3. Keep track of any sales taxes you collected.

4. If you work with one or more partners, make sure everyone gets paid the proper amount.

5. Update your book inventory and re-order as needed.

6. Check your swag inventory and re-order anything you're getting low on.

7. Repair any damaged display items.

8. Repack everything for the next show and stow it in a safe place.

About the Authors

Jeffrey Cook lives in Maple Valley, Washington, with his wife and three large dogs. He was born in Boulder, Colorado, but has lived all over the United States. He's the author of the *Dawn of Steam* trilogy of alternate-history/emergent Steampunk epistolary novels, the YA urban fantasy series *The Fair Folk Chronicles*, and the YA Sci-fi thriller *Mina Cortez: From Bouquets to Bullets*. He's a founding contributing author of Writerpunk Press and has also contributed to a number of role-playing game books for Deep7 Press out of Seattle. When not reading, researching, or writing, Jeffrey enjoys role-playing games and watching football.

Lee French lives in Olympia, WA, and is the author of several fantasy and science fiction books, most notably the *Maze Beset* Trilogy, *The Greatest Sin* series (co-authored with Erik Kort), and assorted tales in her fantasy setting, Ilauris. She's an avid gamer and active member of the Myth-Weavers online RPG community, where she's known for creative squirrel deployment. In addition to spending time there, she also trains year-round for the one-week of glorious madness that is RAGBRAI, has a nice flower garden with one dragon and absolutely no lawn gnomes, and tries in vain every year to grow vegetables that don't get devoured by neighborhood wildlife.

She is an active member of the Northwest Independent Writer's Association and serves as the Municipal Liaison for the Olympia region of NaNoWriMo. Her appearances to date include GenCon, WorldCon, Norwescon, and several other Pacific Northwest sci-fi and fantasy conventions.

Books by the Authors

Urban Fantasy
Fair Folk Chronicles
Jeffrey Cook & Katherine Perkins
Young adult faeries in Seattle
Foul Is Fair
Street Fair
A Fair Fight
All's Fair (Summer 2016)

Spirit Knights series
Lee French
Young adult ghost hunting in Portland
Girls Can't Be Knights
Backyard Dragons
Ethereal Entanglements (Summer 2016)

Angel's Grace trilogy
Jeffrey Cook & AJ Downey
War between angels and demons
Airs & Graces
There But For the Grace
A Coup de Grace (Winter 2016)

Science Fiction

Dawn of Steam trilogy
Jeffrey Cook & Sarah Symonds
Alternate history steampunk
First Light
Gods of the Sun
Rising Suns

Jeffrey Cook
Young Adult standalone adventure
Mina Cortez: From Bouquets to Bullets

Maze Beset trilogy
Lee French
Superhero conspiracy/thriller
Dragons In Pieces
Dragons In Chains
Dragons In Flight

Lee French
Standalone nanotech thriller
Chowndie (Winter 2016)

Fantasy

The Greatest Sin series
Lee French & Erik Kort
Epic snark fantasy
The Fallen
Harbinger
Moon Shades

Tales of Ilauris
Lee French
Standalone fantasy novels
Damsel In Distress
Shadow & Spice (short story)
Al-Kabar

Anthology Appearances

Jeffrey Cook
Sound & Fury: Shakespeare Goes Punk
Once More Unto the Breach: Shakespeare Goes Punk 2
Asylum: A NIWA Anthology
Steampunk Trails #2
Merely This and Nothing More: Poe Goes Punk (Summer 2016)

Lee French
Into the Woods: a fantasy anthology
Merely This and Nothing More: Poe Goes Punk (Summer 2016)
Missing Pieces VII (August 2016)

*9 7 8 1 9 4 4 3 3 4 0 3 1 *